ORIN MARIX

# Democracy Under Siege

*Unmasking the Hidden Threats and Charting a Path to Renewal in the Age of Polarization*

# Contents

# Introduction

I n an era where democracy appears more fragile than ever, the pressing question arises: can we still believe in its promise for the future? This inquiry captures the urgency and critical nature of our current political climate, where democratic principles seem to be at an unprecedented crossroads. Our world is witnessing a seismic shift, with established norms of governance being tested and scrutinized like never before. From the rise of authoritarianism to the pervasive spread of misinformation, the threats facing modern democracies are both complex and deeply rooted.

The urgency of this discussion cannot be overstated. As political divisions deepen across the globe, trust in institutions continues to wane at an alarming rate. In countries once considered stalwarts of democracy, citizens find themselves questioning the very foundations upon which their societies were built. The rapidly changing societal landscape, driven by technological advancements and global interconnectivity, adds layers of complexity to these challenges. As we grapple with such transformative times, understanding the threats to democracy—and the pathways to safeguarding it—has become a crucial pursuit.

This book serves as a guide through this intricate and often unsettling terrain. Organized into ten insightful chapters, it offers a comprehensive exploration of the democratic crisis we face today. Each chapter delves into different facets of this issue, from the increasing polarization of politics to the profound impact of technology on democratic processes. Through a meticulous examination of these topics, the book aims to illuminate the underlying causes of the current democratic malaise and, ultimately, to propose actionable solutions for renewal.

Polarization, a central theme of our analysis, has emerged as one of the most visible symptoms of democratic distress. Political ideologies have hardened, transforming healthy debate into entrenched division. This polarization not only affects government policy but also seeps into the social fabric, influencing how individuals perceive and interact with one another. The consequences are pervasive, leading to gridlock in decision-making bodies and fostering an environment where compromise becomes a relic of the past.

Compounding these issues is the role of technology, which has dramatically reshaped the democratic landscape. While digital platforms have empowered voices previously marginalized, they have also become vectors for misinformation and manipulation. Social media, with its algorithms designed for engagement rather than accuracy, often amplifies extreme views and deepens societal divides. The challenge lies in harnessing these tools for democratic gain while mitigating their potential for harm.

Yet, amidst these daunting challenges, there remain glimmers of hope. Embedded within each chapter are stories of resilience and innovation, highlighting communities and movements that are pushing back against the tides of democratic decay. From grassroots campaigns advocating for electoral reform to technological initiatives promoting transparency and accountability, these examples serve as reminders that change is possible.

As we journey through this exploration, it's imperative to remember that democracy thrives on active engagement. Every citizen's participation and awareness are vital components in shaping its future. The strength of democracy lies not just in its institutions but in the collective will of its people. By understanding the nuances of the current crisis, readers are encouraged to reflect on their roles in supporting and revitalizing democratic ideals.

This book seeks to inspire action and foster engagement, urging readers to go beyond passive observation. It poses challenging questions, encouraging introspection about personal responsibilities and community involvement. The hope is to ignite a renewed commitment to democratic principles, urging individuals to consider how they might contribute to this global endeavor.

The path forward may appear daunting, yet it is navigable through informed action and persistent advocacy. While this book paints a realistic picture of the challenges ahead, it simultaneously offers a vision for renewal—a vision grounded in practical solutions and collaborative efforts. By embracing the spirit of engaged citizenship, we can collectively steer democracy toward a more robust and inclusive future.

Ultimately, this book calls upon politically engaged individuals, academics, and students alike to partake in this critical discourse. Whether you're a seasoned political analyst or someone seeking a deeper understanding of current dynamics, the insights contained within these pages aim to enrich your perspective and equip you with the knowledge required to effect meaningful change.

As we delve into these discussions, let us carry forward the conviction that democracy's promise still holds relevance and vitality. Despite the obstacles, the potential for reinvigoration exists when we choose to engage thoughtfully and act decisively. With concerted effort and shared determination, it is indeed possible to craft a democratic future worthy of belief and trust.

In conclusion, this exploration is not merely academic; it is a call to action. Let us proceed with the understanding that democratic vitality relies on our vigilance and resolve. The journey begins here, inviting each reader to explore, question, and ultimately contribute to the ongoing dialogue about the future of democracy.

# Understanding Democratic Vulnerabilities

U nderstanding democratic vulnerabilities is a matter of recognizing the various threats that challenge the very foundations of governance built on equality, freedom, and justice. These principles are crucial for maintaining societies where citizens actively participate in decision-making processes and ensure governmental accountability. However, these ideals are under constant threat from both internal and external forces that can compromise their integrity. Political polarization, misinformation, and declining trust in institutions have emerged as significant risks to democracy's stability. These vulnerabilities highlight the precarious nature of democracy in today's world, where even established systems are not immune to erosion.

This chapter will delve into the multifaceted threats facing modern democracies, examining how these challenges manifest across different political landscapes. Readers will explore early indicators of democratic erosion, such as waning public confidence and increased partisanship, which can create environments ripe for authoritarian tendencies. The role of a free press, civic participation, and the rule of law in safeguarding democratic frameworks will be discussed, providing insights into the mechanisms that preserve or threaten these systems. Further, the chapter will investigate how economic inequality and technological advancements intersect with political dynamics, potentially exacerbating existing issues within democracies. By analyzing case studies and historical contexts, the discussion aims to uncover patterns that illuminate the fragility of democratic institutions. Each section contributes to a comprehensive understanding of how democracies can adapt to and resist these pressures. Through this examination, the audience gains awareness of the pressing need for proactive measures in fortifying democratic values against ongoing and future challenges.

## Overview of Democratic Principles

Democracy, often lauded as the ideal system of governance, is fundamentally built on principles that emphasize equality, freedom, and justice. At its core, democracy ensures that citizens have equal opportunities to participate in government decision-making processes, regardless of their background or socio-economic status. This inclusive participation is not just a privilege but a right that forms the bedrock of democratic societies. According to Day (2022), the very essence of democracy allows people to chart the course of their government through active involvement, whether in direct or representative forms. By doing so, democracy pushes back against tyranny and authoritarianism, acting as a protective shield by enforcing checks and balances within political systems.

Checks and balances are crucial for maintaining democratic integrity. Without these safeguards, there's a risk of power consolidating in the hands of a few, potentially leading to authoritarian rule. McDermott (2023) highlights the importance of ensuring that elected officials are held accountable, and this is achievable through institutional structures like independent courts and a free press. The diffusion of power across multiple branches of government not only prevents abuse but also fosters an environment where policy decisions undergo scrutiny and debate. Such a mechanism ensures that no single entity can dominate, maintaining power evenly distributed among different institutional bodies.

Active civic participation plays a vital role in keeping governments accountable and resilient against threats to democracy. When citizens engage in discourse, debate, and electoral processes, they reinforce the legitimacy of democratic systems. Civic activism often acts as the first line of defense against potential democratic erosion. For instance, citizens campaigning for policy change or participating in peaceful protests demonstrate democracy's capacity to address societal issues collectively. This engagement underscores the idea that democracy thrives when citizens actively engage with and hold their governments accountable.

However, the act of participation extends beyond mere voting. It encompasses ongoing dialogue between politicians and citizens, ensuring that leaders remain responsive to public needs. Such interaction helps build trust and transparency, key components in reinforcing democratic values. Encouraging civic groups and NGOs to voice concerns without fear of retribution further strengthens civil society's role in democratic health. For example, grassroots movements advocating for social justice reforms remind governments of their responsibility to uphold principles of equality and fairness.

The rule of law is another cornerstone supporting democratic frameworks. It guarantees all citizens receive fair treatment while holding governmental authorities to the same standards. Incorporating a robust legal framework ensures transparent legal proceedings and impartial judgments, deterring potential abuses of power. As Day (2022) emphasizes, protecting human rights and maintaining equality before the law prevent any segment of society from being marginalized or unjustly treated. In this context, the legal system operates not only to adjudicate disputes but also to protect human dignity and promote equitable access to justice for all.

Significantly, the rule of law also provides mechanisms for self-correction within democracies. Democratic institutions possess inherent capacities to identify flaws and implement necessary reforms. This adaptability demonstrates democracy's enduring strength: the ability to evolve and better serve its populace. Such resilience is pivotal in times of crisis when swift, decisive action may be required to preserve democratic ideals.

Despite these foundational principles, contemporary democracies face numerous challenges that threaten their stability and efficacy. Political polarization, misinformation, and waning public trust in institutions are pressing issues requiring immediate attention. Addressing such vulnerabilities necessitates not only reaffirming commitment to democratic values but also innovating new solutions to modern problems.

Moreover, embracing technological advancements responsibly can enhance democracy rather than hinder it. While digital platforms enable broader citizen participation and information dissemination, they can also propagate misinformation and deepen divides if left unchecked. Thus, balancing technological growth with safeguarding democratic integrity is essential for future-proofing democracies against emerging threats.

To maintain democracy's vitality, fostering an informed and engaged citizenry remains paramount. Educational initiatives aimed at promoting civic literacy and critical thinking equip individuals with the tools needed to navigate complex political landscapes. These programs should focus on imparting knowledge about democratic structures, political rights, and civic duties, enabling citizens to participate more fully in democratic processes.

International cooperation also plays a significant role in preserving democratic principles. Democracies worldwide must unite to support each other in the face of authoritarian pressure and external threats. Solidarity among democratic nations encourages sharing successful practices, strategies, and innovations, thereby strengthening global democratic resilience.

## Initial Signs of Vulnerability in Democratic Systems

Early indicators of democratic erosion are critical for understanding the dynamics that threaten the stability of democratic systems. Among these indicators, declining trust in government entities stands out as a fundamental concern. When citizens lose faith in their leaders and institutions, it creates a fertile ground for apathy and disillusionment with democratic processes. This erosion of trust can lead people to question the legitimacy of elected officials and the effectiveness of governance, weakening public engagement and participation in democratic activities (Saskia Brechenmacher & Saskia Brechenmacher, 2019). Historical contexts reinforce this notion; periods of low confidence in government often coincide with increased political turmoil and societal unrest.

Moreover, increased partisanship is another significant early warning sign of democratic erosion. Political landscapes dominated by extreme partisan divides create environments filled with hostility and mistrust between opposing factions. This heightened polarization makes bipartisan cooperation exceedingly difficult, weakening policy-making and impeding the government's ability to address national challenges effectively. Milan W. Svolik noted that such intense divides contribute to an atmosphere where political opponents are seen not just as rivals but as enemies, exacerbating tensions and undermining democratic norms (Ugarte, n.d.).

Attacks on press freedom also signal potential threats to democracy. A free press serves as both a watchdog and a crucial platform for public discourse, ensuring transparency and accountability in governance. However, when media freedoms are curtailed, either through direct censorship or subtle forms of control, it limits the flow of information necessary for informed citizenry. This suppression of journalistic independence can skew public perception and narrative, ultimately eroding trust between the populace and their leaders. In societies where press freedom is compromised, citizens may struggle to access reliable news, making them more vulnerable to misinformation and manipulation.

Voter disenfranchisement poses another substantial threat to democratic integrity by skewing political representation. Policies designed to suppress or restrict certain groups from voting can marginalize large sections of the electorate, depriving them of their voice in the democratic process. This systemic inequality distorts election outcomes and leads to governance that does not accurately reflect the will of all its constituents, thereby undermining the very foundation of democracy. Disenfranchisement practices, whether through stringent voter ID laws or gerrymandering, highlight efforts to dilute the influence of particular demographics, often based on racial, socioeconomic, or political lines.

Trust in democratic institutions is essential for their effective functioning. As history has shown, once this trust diminishes, so too does the moral authority of those institutions. The decline in trust has been documented extensively across Western democracies, where surveys report falling confidence in political parties and government bodies. This phenomenon has been linked to the rise of populist movements that exploit public dissatisfaction, further weakening traditional political structures (Saskia Brechenmacher & Saskia Brechenmacher, 2019). In essence, when citizens no longer believe that democratic institutions serve their interests, they are less likely to participate in civic engagement, creating a cycle of disengagement and decay.

Efforts to counteract these trends must focus on rebuilding trust through transparency, accountability, and inclusivity. Encouraging open dialogue between government officials and citizens can help bridge the gap created by distrust, while policies that prioritize fairness and equality in representation may restore faith in democratic processes. Addressing partisanship requires promoting a political culture that values compromise and mutual respect, fostering an environment where diverse perspectives can collaborate towards common goals.

Recognizing and supporting press freedom is vital for preserving an informed electorate. Media outlets must be able to operate without undue influence or restriction, allowing journalists to report accurately and objectively. By safeguarding these freedoms, societies ensure that citizens have access to a broad spectrum of viewpoints and the necessary information to make educated decisions about their leaders and policies. Furthermore, combatting voter disenfranchisement involves advocating for reforms that guarantee equal access to voting for all citizens. Ensuring that every eligible voter can exercise their right without obstacles is fundamental for maintaining the integrity of democratic elections.

## Relevance in Today's Political Climate

The democratic landscape faces significant challenges as authoritarian regimes rise, intertwining with global economic disparities. Economic inequality often emerges as a root cause for the flourishing of such regimes, given that it marginalizes large segments of society, creating dissatisfaction and unrest. This frustration can lead to the election of leaders who promise swift solutions through centralized power—a hallmark of authoritarian governance. As economic divides widen, they contribute to the erosion of democratic structures by facilitating environments ripe for antidemocratic sentiments. For instance, the post-2008 financial crisis saw populist movements gain momentum, exploiting public disillusionment with existing democratic processes and leading to the election of illiberal leaders in various parts of Europe and the Americas (Schleffer & Miller, 2021).

Examining specific case studies reveals the fragility of democratic institutions in the face of political upheaval. Take, for example, Venezuela, where economic mismanagement led to widespread poverty, fueling political unrest and enabling authoritarian practices under Nicolás Maduro. Similarly, Hungary's slide into an illiberal state showcases how democracies can be dismantled from within through constitutional manipulations and suppression of opposing voices. These cases highlight critical lessons, emphasizing the need for robust economic policies and vigilant civil societies that can hold governments accountable while offering insight into potential democratic restoration strategies.

In today's media landscape, diverse outlets play a crucial role in shaping political narratives. While they provide platforms for free speech, they also facilitate misinformation campaigns that distort democratic processes. Social media, in particular, has become both a tool for empowerment and a weapon of division. Its use in spreading false information was notably evident during the 2016 U.S. presidential election and Brexit referendum, illustrating the weakening effect misleading content can have on established democratic regimes (Schleffer & Miller, 2021). The rapid dissemination of unfounded claims undermines public trust in democratic institutions and heightens societal divisions. Thus, understanding social media's impact is vital for developing safeguards against its misuse.

Moreover, youth engagement remains a beacon of hope amidst these challenges. Young generations are increasingly vocal about their demands for democratic reform and rights, spurred by a heightened awareness of global injustices. Their activism brings renewed energy to democratic systems, urging them towards inclusivity and responsiveness to modern-day issues. From climate change protests to movements against systemic racism, young people drive reforms—insisting on accountability and transparency in governance. Their involvement in politics rejuvenates democracy, pushing for systems that reflect contemporary values and aspirations.

Addressing democratic vulnerabilities requires acknowledging these complex, interconnected factors. While the rise of authoritarianism globally poses a significant threat, case studies offer valuable lessons. They highlight the necessity for strong economic policies, media literacy, and active civic participation as bulwarks against autocratic tendencies. Furthermore, empowering young people to take part in governance not only revitalizes democratic structures but also ensures their resilience against future threats. By fostering an inclusive dialogue, integrating multiple perspectives, and reinforcing democratic norms, societies can chart a course towards more robust democratic systems resistant to authoritarian encroachment.

Ultimately, safeguarding democracy calls for a coordinated effort across borders. Democratic nations must align around core democratic principles while adapting domestic policies to counter both internal and external threats. International cooperation, grounded in shared values, can effectively support the global struggle for democratic ideals. Democracy's inherent flexibility allows it to adapt to changing circumstances, drawing strength from diverse voices united in pursuit of freedom and justice.

## Framework for the Book's Analysis

In recent years, democracies around the world have been facing unprecedented challenges that threaten their very foundations. To truly understand these threats, it is crucial to adopt a holistic approach that considers the interplay of political, social, and economic factors. Democracy does not operate in a vacuum; it is influenced by various interconnected elements that contribute to its vulnerabilities. For instance, intense political polarization can lead to societal divisions, which are often exacerbated by economic inequality and social unrest. This creates an environment where democratic norms can be easily eroded, as seen in many countries experiencing rising populism (Ziblatt, 2023).

This book will explore these challenges through a thematic organization of chapters, facilitating a clear comprehension of specific themes related to the threats democracy faces today. By doing so, readers can systematically delve into each area of concern, from political polarization to economic disparities, understanding how each aspect interlinks with others to form a complex web of challenges. Such a structured approach ensures that the analysis remains focused and coherent, allowing for a deeper exploration of the issues at hand. The thematic divisions also help in highlighting the interplay between global and local dynamics, demonstrating how international trends influence domestic politics and vice versa.

A key aspect of this book is its reliance on data-driven analysis, which provides evidence-based credibility to the discussions. By utilizing case studies, statistical data, trends, and historical contexts, we aim to present a comprehensive picture of democratic threats. For example, we will examine the rise of populist movements in different regions and analyze their impact on democratic institutions. These case studies serve as tangible examples of how theoretical concepts play out in real-world scenarios, offering insights into the mechanisms behind democratic decline (*Democratic Threats and Resilience | Einaudi Center*, 2024).

Furthermore, this analytical framework helps debunk myths and misperceptions about democracy's resilience. By presenting factual evidence and real-world examples, we underscore the urgency of addressing these threats proactively. The historical context provided will show how similar challenges were faced and mitigated in the past, offering lessons that can inform current strategies. Understanding these patterns is crucial for anticipating potential outcomes and designing effective interventions.

One of the standout features of this book is its emphasis on policy-focused solutions. It's not enough to simply identify the problems; actionable steps must be taken to address them. Throughout the chapters, we will highlight policies that have proven effective in strengthening democratic institutions and propose new ones tailored to contemporary challenges. Initiatives like electoral reforms, participatory governance models, and civic education programs are explored for their potential to reinvigorate democratic processes and enhance citizen engagement.

Moreover, the book seeks to bridge the gap between theory and practice, empowering readers to effect change in their communities. By providing practical recommendations, we hope to inspire action among politically engaged individuals and scholars who wish to contribute to democratic renewal. This empowerment is vital, as it transforms passive observers into active participants in safeguarding democratic values. Encouraging grassroots movements and fostering dialogue among diverse groups are essential strategies to counter authoritarian tendencies and promote inclusivity.

## Objectives and Reader Insights

In our increasingly interconnected world, understanding the complexities of democratic challenges is paramount for all citizens. This book aims to illuminate the vulnerabilities facing democracies today and provide readers with the insights necessary to navigate these turbulent times effectively. By examining various facets such as cultural, economic, and technological influences, we expose the nuanced layers that threaten democratic systems globally. The goal of this subpoint is to articulate how informed citizenship, combined with a comprehension of the underlying threats, contributes to a more robust democratic society.

Informed citizenship is the bedrock of democracy, fostering an environment where individuals can actively participate in democratic processes. Recognizing the root causes of contemporary democratic challenges is essential for citizens to engage meaningfully and responsibly. For instance, when citizens understand how technological advancements impact electoral integrity, they become more vigilant against misinformation and cyber interference. Similarly, awareness of economic disparities brings attention to how inequality might fuel populism and authoritarian tendencies. These insights equip citizens to hold political leaders accountable and advocate for policies that uphold democratic values (WUTTKE & FOOS, 2024).

Exploring the multifaceted nature of democratic vulnerabilities necessitates examining a range of factors contributing to their fragility. Culturally, the shifting paradigms of societal values can both strengthen and weaken democratic frameworks. While pluralism and diversity are cornerstones of liberal democracy, they may also become targets for populist rhetoric, undermining social cohesion. Economically, global financial crises have demonstrated how fragile economies can destabilize governments, making them susceptible to both internal dissent and external manipulation. Technologically, the rapid dissemination of information, while democratizing in nature, often challenges established norms by propagating falsehoods and creating echo chambers that skew public perception. Each of these factors is crucial in painting a comprehensive picture of democracy's vulnerabilities and underscores the need for vigilance and adaptability among its defenders (Kleinfeld, 2022).

Actionable recommendations are vital in guiding proactive participation and fortifying democratic systems against potential erosion. Encouraging citizen engagement goes beyond mere voting; it involves active involvement in community dialogues, policy deliberations, and civic initiatives that drive positive change. Educating citizens on media literacy helps them discern credible sources from disinformation, enabling informed decision-making. Furthermore, fostering cross-generational conversations around democratic values ensures that younger generations are equipped to carry forward the torch of democratic ideals. By implementing these strategies, individuals contribute to building a resilient democracy capable of withstanding both current and future challenges (WUTTKE & FOOS, 2024).

Stressing shared responsibility highlights the collective role each citizen plays in safeguarding democracy. Democratic governance thrives when individuals recognize their duty not only as voters but as custodians of democratic values. This sense of shared responsibility strengthens societal bonds and encourages collaborative efforts to address systemic issues. For example, when citizens collectively demand transparency and accountability from their leaders, it catalyzes reforms that enhance democratic integrity. Such shared initiatives reflect the core principle that democracy is not the sole responsibility of elected officials but of every individual within the society (Kleinfeld, 2022).

# Concluding Thoughts

The chapter elaborates on the pressing threats faced by contemporary democracies and underscores their significance. It highlights the erosion of trust in government institutions, increased political polarization, and attacks on press freedom as major challenges. These issues endanger democratic integrity, causing citizens to question the legitimacy of elected officials and decreasing civic engagement. The rise of misinformation and voter disenfranchisement further compounds these problems, skewing political representation and weakening democratic structures. This analysis serves as a sobering reminder of how fragile democratic institutions can be in the face of multifaceted pressures.

This examination aims to raise awareness among readers about current democratic challenges, encouraging them to appreciate the complexity of these issues. By understanding the interconnected social, economic, and political influences threatening democratic systems, individuals and academics can better advocate for solutions that reinforce democratic resilience. Addressing these vulnerabilities requires vigilance, proactive citizenship, and embracing inclusive dialogues aimed at fostering transparency and accountability. While taking into account historical lessons and case studies, the chapter emphasizes that safeguarding democracy is a collective responsibility—one that demands sustained commitment and adaptability from all who cherish its principles.

# Reference List

*Democratic Threats and Resilience | Einaudi Center.* (2024, June 5). Einaudi.cornell.edu. https://einaudi.cornell.edu/research/democratic-threats-and-resilience

Day, J. (2022, April 12). *14 Principles of Democracy.* Liberties.eu; Liberties.

https://www.liberties.eu/en/stories/principles-of-democracy/44151

Kleinfeld, R. (2022, September 15). *Five Strategies to Support U.S. Democracy*. Carnegie Endowment for International Peace. https://carnegieendowment. org/2022/09/15/five-strategies-to-support-u.s.-democracy-pub-87918

McDermott, S. (2023, March 24). *A Civil Society Declaration of Democratic Principles on the Occasion of the 2023 Summit for Democracy*. McCain Institute. https://www.mccaininstitute.org/resources/in-the-news/a-civil-society-declaration-of-democratic-principles-on-the-occasion-of-the-2023-sum mit-for-democracy/

Repucci, S., & Slipowitz, A. (2022). *The Global Expansion of Authoritarian Rule*. Freedom House; Freedom House. https://freedomhouse.org/report/ freedom-world/2022/global-expansion-authoritarian-rule

Saskia Brechenmacher, & Saskia Brechenmacher. (2019). *Comparing Democratic Distress in the United States and Europe*. Carnegie Endowment for International Peace. https://carnegieendowment.org/2018/06/21/compar ing-democratic-distress-in-united-states-and-europe-pub-76646

Schleffer, G., & Miller, B. (2021). *The Political Effects of Social Media Platforms on Different Regime Types*. Texas National Security Review. https://t nsr.org/2021/07/the-political-effects-of-social-media-platforms-on-diffe rent-regime-types/

Ugarte, R. (n.d.). *The United States Has a Democracy Problem: What Democratic*

*Erosion Scholarship Tells Us about January 6.* Items. https://items.ssrc.org/democracy-papers/the-united-states-has-a-democracy-problem-what-democratic-erosion-scholarship-tells-us-about-january-6/

WUTTKE, A., & FOOS, F. (2024, June 27). *Making the case for democracy: A field-experiment on democratic persuasion.* European Journal of Political Research; Wiley. https://doi.org/10.1111/1475-6765.12705

Ziblatt, D. (2023). *Challenges to Democracy.* Scholar.harvard.edu. https://scholar.harvard.edu/dziblatt/challenges-democracy

# Polarization and Its Consequences

Political polarization is a formidable force disrupting democratic norms worldwide. It deepens divisions within societies and erodes the foundational principles critical for effective governance. In many democracies, individuals increasingly identify with rigid ideological stances, perceiving opposing views as direct threats to their values and identities. This intensification of partisan allegiances transforms political discourse into a battleground, where compromise becomes elusive and agreements are scarce. As these divides grow, citizens often find themselves in echo chambers that amplify biases and distort perceptions of reality. The relentless vigor of such polarization poses significant challenges to collective decision-making processes in democratic settings.

This chapter delves into the nuanced consequences of extreme political polarization, particularly its detrimental impact on democratic norms. Readers will explore how historical events have laid the groundwork for current divides, highlighting pivotal shifts like realignments in party affiliations following landmark legislation. Furthermore, the discussion extends to cultural conflicts that act as catalysts for deeper societal rifts, focusing on contentious issues such as abortion and immigration. By examining the role of media in shaping public perception and reinforcing ideological divides, the narrative underscores how sensationalism exacerbates polarization. Additionally, it considers the implications of legislative gridlock, which stagnates policy developments and undermines democratic governance. Finally, the chapter offers a comparative analysis of international examples, providing insights into diverse approaches to mitigating political polarization and maintaining democratic integrity. Through this exploration, readers will gain a comprehensive understanding of how polarization permeates various aspects of political life, challenging the resilience of democratic institutions globally.

## Historical Context of Political Polarization

In the United States, political polarization has roots that can be traced back through a tapestry of historical events and societal shifts. Various pivotal moments have intensified divisions and cemented partisan identities over time. For instance, the Civil Rights Movement of the 1960s reshaped political allegiances, pushing many former Southern Democrats towards the Republican Party (Kleinfeld, 2023). The impact was profound, as racial prejudice became a key factor in party identification. This ideological sorting marked the beginning of a prolonged phase of deepening political divides.

As America's cultural landscape continued to evolve, ensuing decades witnessed further entrenchment of partisan lines. The Vietnam War, Watergate scandal, and ongoing debates over women's rights, gay rights, and environmental protections added layers of complexity to the existing political narrative (How Did Political Polarization Begin, and Where Does It End?, n.d.). These cultural cleavages were more than mere policy differences; they touched on personal values and identity, making compromise increasingly challenging.

A significant portion of this growing ideological divide can be attributed to major legislation that has shaped partisan conflict. Policies like the Civil Rights Act of 1964 set in motion a realignment of party affiliations that has continued to develop over the decades. As legislative battles raged, new policies concerning health care, taxation, and gun control regularly sparked fierce partisan debates. Each piece of legislation not only addressed immediate issues but also further defined the boundaries between opposing political factions.

The global landscape provides additional context for understanding these shifts in U.S. politics. By looking beyond American borders, we can see similar trends unfolding across other democratic societies. European nations, for example, have experienced their own waves of political polarization. In countries like France and Italy, the rise of populist movements mirrors the intensification of division seen in the United States. Populists often challenge existing political norms by appealing directly to citizens' fears and frustrations, thereby exacerbating divides within the populace.

Comparatively, Nordic countries present a contrasting approach to managing polarization. These nations have traditionally emphasized consensus-building practices and robust social welfare policies, which help mitigate extreme political divides. Their models demonstrate that even within polarized environments, strategic governance approaches can foster unity and preserve democratic norms.

Despite these divergent paths, one consistent theme emerges: the role of media in shaping political boundaries is undeniable. In recent decades, media landscapes have transformed dramatically, with social media platforms playing a particularly influential role. The proliferation of online echo chambers allows individuals to curate their information consumption, often reinforcing existing biases and accelerating polarization (Kleinfeld, 2023).

The interplay between media and politics has been especially evident in events such as the Arab Spring and the January 6 assault on the U.S. Capitol. Initially hailed for democratizing information flow, social media's potential to disrupt political hierarchies quickly turned into a double-edged sword. Scandals involving data manipulation and misinformation campaigns highlighted how these tools could deepen existing divides rather than encourage dialogue or understanding.

As we draw parallels between the American experience and global trends, a few critical questions arise for democratic societies worldwide. How can democracies maintain effective governance amid rising polarization? What strategies might allow for productive discourse and constructive policymaking? While there are no easy answers, drawing insights from both domestic history and international examples could offer pathways forward.

# Cultural Wars and Political Discourse

In the contemporary political landscape, cultural conflicts have emerged as potent drivers of polarization, fundamentally altering public discourse and societal cohesion. These cultural wars often revolve around hot-button issues such as abortion and immigration, which are deeply rooted in ideological divides that shape and intensify polarization. As these topics become battlefields for opposing viewpoints, they contribute to a widespread erosion of social trust, making compromise and understanding increasingly elusive.

The issue of abortion, for instance, is a deeply personal and moral dilemma, yet it is frequently reduced to a binary argument within the political arena. This reductionism simplifies complex ethical considerations into rigid policy positions, forcing individuals to align with one side or the other. Such polarizing stances create an unbridgeable chasm between groups who might otherwise find common ground. As a result, societal discourse becomes less about understanding diverse perspectives and more about defending one's ideological territory. A similar pattern is observed in debates surrounding immigration, where the conversation often devolves into an "us versus them" narrative. The portrayal of immigrants, either as threats to national security or as victims in need of protection, reflects deep-seated ideological differences that exacerbate political polarization. When these issues are used as cultural rallying cries, they not only deepen existing divisions but also hinder productive dialogue and problem-solving.

Media outlets play a pivotal role in framing these cultural narratives, and their shift towards sensationalism has further fueled polarization. In an era where clickbait headlines and 24-hour news cycles dominate, nuanced discussions are often sacrificed for attention-grabbing soundbites. Media channels, driven by the imperative to maintain viewer engagement, tend to amplify extreme voices while marginalizing moderate perspectives. This creates a feedback loop, where sensational coverage reinforces polarized views, encouraging the public to adopt more entrenched and adversarial positions. The implications of this media-driven polarization extend beyond mere perception; they influence electoral outcomes and policymaking processes. When cultural issues are framed in stark, divisive terms, political leaders may feel pressured to adopt uncompromising stances to satisfy their constituencies. This, in turn, can lead to legislative stalemate and hinder effective governance, as policymakers prioritize ideological purity over pragmatic solutions.

Cultural wars also play a significant role in shaping political identity formation. For many individuals, allegiance to a particular stance on cultural issues becomes intertwined with their sense of self and community. This phenomenon is particularly evident in the practice of identity politics, where personal beliefs and values are seen as integral components of one's political identity. Cultural war issues often resonate at a deeply personal level, compelling individuals to participate actively in these conflicts. The stakes are not merely political but existential, as people perceive their participation as a defense of their core values and way of life. Consequently, political identities become increasingly defined by opposition to those who hold differing views, perpetuating cycles of polarization.

Moreover, the personal nature of these cultural conflicts can incapacitate dialogue and compromise. When political adversaries are viewed not just as opponents but as existential threats, it becomes difficult to engage in constructive conversations. Instead, political discourse is replaced by a zero-sum game, where the victory of one side necessarily entails the defeat of the other. This mindset fosters a climate of distrust and hostility, undermining the foundations of democratic deliberation and cooperation.

As cultural conflicts continue to shape political landscapes, potential interventions must be considered to mitigate their polarizing effects. Strategies could include promoting diverse and inclusive dialogues that encourage empathy and understanding between opposing groups. Educational initiatives aimed at increasing digital literacy and critical thinking could help individuals navigate media narratives more thoughtfully. Moreover, fostering environments where nuanced discussion is valued over sensationalism may promote healthier discourse.

## Impact on Compromise and Governance

Polarization in political landscapes has far-reaching consequences on governance and the ability to achieve meaningful compromise. As partisan affiliations become increasingly entrenched, the spirit of bipartisan cooperation has sharply declined, ushering in a new era where gridlock and inefficiency dominate legislative processes. This reduction in cross-party collaboration poses significant challenges to effective governance, as policymakers find it harder to reach consensual agreements that address the diverse needs of the electorate.

In recent decades, trends indicate a marked decline in bipartisan efforts within legislative bodies, a phenomenon driven by ideological purism and party loyalty overshadowing collaborative decision-making. The ramifications are profound: without the ability to negotiate and compromise, policies stagnate, and critical governmental functions falter. Policymakers, once adept at bridging gaps between divergent viewpoints, now often struggle to move past partisan stalemates. Consequently, policies that should have been the result of careful negotiation and mutual concessions instead remain mired in divisive rhetoric and unyielding positions. This lack of compromise undermines democratic norms, weakening institutions that rely on flexibility and adaptability to serve the public effectively (Kleinfeld, 2023).

Legislative gridlock serves as a stark illustration of how polarization impairs governance. When partisan divides deepen, the passage of essential legislation becomes exceedingly difficult, if not impossible. This gridlock manifests in delayed budgets, stalled reforms, and an inability to respond coherently to emergent national issues. In the U.S., for instance, Congress has seen numerous instances where polarized stances led to government shutdowns or reliance on temporary stopgap measures that fail to address underlying problems comprehensively. Such deadlocks diminish the public's faith in democratic systems, as citizens perceive their leaders as unwilling or incapable of fulfilling their legislative responsibilities.

Moreover, legislative gridlock does not merely disrupt immediate governance but also sets a precedent for future interactions among lawmakers.

It fosters an environment where partisan brinkmanship is normalized, further entrenching division and causing long-term harm to democratic functionality. With each episode of gridlock, trust erodes between opposition parties, making future cooperation even more elusive. The cycle of inaction becomes self-perpetuating, with each failure to compromise reinforcing the notion that partisanship is a barrier too formidable to overcome (Pew Research Center, 2014).

Further compounding the issue is the rise of polarized majoritarian rule, which presents significant risks to minority rights and representation. In a highly polarized context, majority groups wield disproportionate power, dominating legislative agendas and sidelining minority voices. This dynamic threatens to marginalize specific communities, stifling diversity of thought and reducing the breadth of perspectives that inform policy decisions. Moreover, when majoritarian rule prevails, it risks creating laws that cater only to the majority's interests, ignoring the needs and concerns of minority groups who may already face systemic disadvantages.

The impacts on minority rights and representation are profound. Policies enacted under such conditions often fail to consider the implications for marginalized groups, leading to inequities and exacerbating existing disparities. For example, majoritarian-driven legislation can undermine protections for racial, religious, or socioeconomic minorities, resulting in legal frameworks that do not reflect the rich pluralism of society. In this way, polarized rule jeopardizes the fundamental tenets of democracy, which are predicated on inclusivity and equitable representation.

Additionally, the erosion of minority rights under polarized governance scenarios can foster social unrest and deteriorate civic trust. As policies become increasingly skewed toward majority preferences, disenfranchised groups may resort to alternative forms of expression, including protests or civil disobedience, to make their voices heard. Such tensions strain the social fabric, potentially escalating into broader conflicts that undermine societal stability and cohesion. Democratic resilience hinges upon the capacity to accommodate diverse opinions, yet polarized majoritarianism diminishes this capability, creating environments ripe for discord and division.

To navigate these challenges, it is imperative to acknowledge the detrimental effects of polarization on governance and work towards mitigating its impact. Encouraging open dialogue and fostering environments where varied perspectives can contribute to the discourse are crucial steps in counteracting divisive tendencies. Building bridges across ideological divides necessitates commitment from policymakers to prioritize common ground over partisan allegiance. By emphasizing shared goals and values, it becomes possible to construct policies that reflect collective aspirations, ensuring that governance remains responsive to all segments of the population.

## Case Studies of Political Polarization

In recent years, political polarization has become a significant concern for democratic governance, manifesting starkly during key political events such as the 2016 U.S. Presidential Election. This election was a hallmark of deep-seated divisions within American society, highlighting how polarized politics can profoundly affect voter behavior and campaign strategies. Candidates relied heavily on divisive rhetoric to galvanize their base, often emphasizing differences rather than shared goals. The electorate split along ideological lines, with each side perceiving the other as an existential threat to their values and way of life. This schism was not merely anecdotal but corroborated by voting statistics, which displayed sharp demographic splits that reflect long-standing social and economic divides.

Furthermore, campaign strategies in 2016 increasingly employed micro-targeting techniques, leveraging data analytics to tailor messages to specific demographic groups. While this approach is technologically sophisticated, it reinforces existing biases by feeding individuals information that confirms their pre-existing beliefs rather than challenging them to consider alternative viewpoints (Gorodnichenko et al., 2021). The incessant focus on sensational headlines and emotionally charged content perpetuated a cycle where voters became more entrenched in their positions, increasing polarization and reducing potential avenues for dialogue and compromise.

Across the Atlantic, Brexit served as a parallel case of polarization in the UK, demonstrating how misinformation can shape public opinion and policy decisions. The Brexit campaign was infamous for its use of dubious claims and misleading statistics that fueled fear and uncertainty amongst the electorate. The portrayal of the European Union as a bureaucratic overlord resonated with those feeling disenfranchised by globalism, driving a wedge between 'Leave' and 'Remain' supporters. Social media platforms played a critical role in disseminating these narratives, often amplified by automated bots that appeared to support grassroots movements but were strategically deployed to sway public perception (Gorodnichenko et al., 2021).

The aftermath of the referendum revealed the depth of societal fracture, with families, communities, and political parties divided over issues of sovereignty, immigration, and national identity. This division has posed ongoing challenges for the UK government, complicating efforts to negotiate coherent exit strategies and maintain domestic unity. As one analyst remarked, the Brexit vote symbolized a broader trend of division across Western democracies, where simplified narratives and populist sentiments overshadow complex realities.

Within the United States, the partisan divide in Congress exemplifies another consequence of polarization. Legislative processes that once depended on bipartisan cooperation have become arenas of conflict, with voting patterns reflecting strict party loyalty rather than deliberative consensus. The increasing rarity of cross-party collaboration has resulted in legislative gridlock, where even pressing national concerns struggle to find solutions due to entrenched partisanship. Leadership within both the Republican and Democratic parties has often reinforced these divisions, focusing on short-term electoral gains rather than long-term policy achievements (Osmundsen et al., 2021).

This environment fosters a winner-takes-all mentality, undermining fundamental democratic norms like compromise and mutual respect. The gridlock not only stalls essential reforms but also erodes public trust in governmental institutions, contributing to political disillusionment. When citizens perceive elected officials as more invested in partisan battles than serving the common good, faith in democracy wanes—a dangerous trend that can destabilize societies and embolden authoritarian tendencies.

Addressing these challenges requires acknowledging the powerful role polarization plays in shaping modern political landscapes. Efforts must be directed towards fostering environments where diverse opinions are discussed constructively and where misinformation is rigorously countered with factual reporting. Educational endeavors aimed at improving media literacy could empower citizens to navigate the complex information ecosystem more effectively, making them less susceptible to manipulative tactics.

## Comparative Analysis with Other Democracies

Political polarization has become a pervasive challenge in democracies worldwide, yet its impact varies significantly across countries. By examining European democracies such as France and Italy, we can gain valuable insights into how political polarization manifests and evolves. These nations have experienced noteworthy shifts due to a rise in populism, which has increasingly tied itself to their polarized political landscapes.

In France, the traditional left-right political spectrum has been disrupted by the emergence of populist figures like Marine Le Pen and her National Rally party. Le Pen's rhetoric focuses on nationalism, anti-immigration, and skepticism towards the European Union, creating stark divides in public opinion and further polarizing the electorate (Gidron, Adams, and Horne, 2022). Similarly, in Italy, the ascent of parties like the Five Star Movement and the League has contributed to heightened polarization. These parties thrive on populist narratives that appeal to disenfranchised voters disillusioned with established political elites. Their success has fueled an environment where political debates are increasingly framed in extreme terms, exacerbating divisions within society.

While polarization is rising in parts of Europe, Nordic countries demonstrate alternative approaches to managing these challenges. Nations like Denmark, Norway, Sweden, and Finland stand out for their consensus-oriented institutions and robust social welfare policies (Bernaerts et al., 2022).

Consensus-building practices, ingrained in their political systems, encourage collaboration across party lines, fostering environments where dialogue and compromise prevent extreme polarization. These countries prioritize policy decisions that emphasize social equity and citizen wellbeing, mitigating the divisiveness often seen in other democracies. Furthermore, the strong welfare state model ensures a safety net that reduces economic inequalities, a known driver of polarization. This approach highlights the potential for social cohesion in counteracting divisive political trends.

The type of electoral system in place also plays a critical role in shaping political polarization. In majoritarian systems like first-past-the-post (FPTP), prevalent in countries like the United States and the United Kingdom, winner-takes-all outcomes often lead to two-party dominance. This setup can intensify polarization by marginalizing smaller parties and discouraging nuanced discourse. As political power becomes concentrated around two dominant parties, the middle ground diminishes, polarizing debates further (Davis et al., 2024).

On the other hand, countries employing proportional representation (PR) tend to exhibit lower levels of polarization. PR allows for multiple parties to gain representation proportional to their share of the vote, encouraging coalition governments and greater political pluralism. The presence of multiple voices in parliament necessitates negotiation and cooperation, reducing adversarial politics. This electoral design is evident in many Scandinavian nations, where diverse parties contribute to balanced governance, preventing any single ideology from dominating the political landscape.

In reviewing these contrasting dynamics, it becomes clear that institutional frameworks significantly influence the degree of polarization within a country. Populism, while playing a role in escalating divisions, interacts with these institutional structures to varying extents. The Nordic model illustrates how democratic norms can withstand polarization through inclusive policies and consensus-building. Conversely, the experiences of countries like France and Italy underscore the volatility of populism in disrupting established political orders.

Understanding these international variations sheds light on possible strategies for addressing polarization in other contexts. For politically engaged audiences and scholars, examining how different democracies navigate these challenges deepens comprehension of the factors driving polarization. Moreover, it suggests pathways that might mitigate its consequences, emphasizing the importance of institutional resilience and social policies in maintaining democratic health.

## Summary and Reflections

As discussed throughout this chapter, political polarization deeply challenges democratic norms by highlighting the stark divisions that have developed over time. Historical events and cultural conflicts have played significant roles in widening these gaps, making compromise increasingly difficult. From legislative gridlock to polarized media narratives, each element adds to a complex web of partisanship that threatens the effective functioning of democratic governance. Partisan identities have grown more pronounced with major legislation and cultural wars further entrenching ideological divides. This environment not only limits the ability for constructive dialogue but also endangers the rights of minority groups as majority parties dominate the political landscape.

Moreover, the impact of media sensationalism and social echo chambers exacerbates these divides, influencing both electoral outcomes and policy decisions. The struggles of other democracies serve as cautionary tales, while Nordic countries offer examples of consensus-building efforts that manage to maintain some degree of unity. However, the pervasive nature of polarization continues to pose questions about the resilience and adaptability of democratic systems. Finding solutions within this challenging context is essential, yet the path forward remains unclear amidst deep-seated divides that fracture societal cohesion and compromise democratic integrity.

# Reference List

Bernaerts, K., Blanckaert, B., & Caluwaerts, D. (2022, September 30). *Institutional design and polarization. Do consensus democracies fare better in fighting polarization than majoritarian democracies?* Democratization. https://doi.org/10.1080/13510347.2022.2117300

Davis, B., Goodliffe, J., & Hawkins, K. (2024, March 12). *The Two-Way Effects of Populism on Affective Polarization.* Comparative Political Studies; SAGE Publishing. https://doi.org/10.1177/00104140241237453

Gorodnichenko, Y., Pham, T., & Talavera, O. (2021, July). *Social media, sentiment and public opinions: Evidence from #Brexit and #USElection.* European Economic Review. https://doi.org/10.1016/j.euroecorev.2021.103772

*How Did Political Polarization Begin, and Where Does it End?* (n.d.). Impact | Giving to Duke. https://impact.duke.edu/story/how-did-political-polariza tion-begin-and-where-does-it-end

Kleinfeld, R. (2023). *Polarization, Democracy, and Political Violence in the United States: What the Research Says.* Carnegie Endowment for International Peace. https://carnegieendowment.org/research/2023/09/polarization-democra cy-and-political-violence-in-the-united-states-what-the-research-says

Osmundsen, M., Bang Petersen, M., & Bor, A. (2021, May 13). *How partisan polarization drives the spread of fake news.* Brookings. https://www .brookings.edu/articles/how-partisan-polarization-drives-the-spread-of-fake-news/


Pew Research Center. (2014, June 12). *Political Polarization in the American Public*. Pew Research Center. https://www.pewresearch.org/politics/2014/06/12/political-polarization-in-the-american-public/


West, D. M. (2024, November 7). *How disinformation defined the 2024 election narrative*. Brookings. https://www.brookings.edu/articles/how-disinformation-defined-the-2024-election-narrative/

# Social Media and Disinformation

Social media's influence on the spread of disinformation is a matter of growing concern. With the evolution of communication technologies, social platforms have become crucial players in how information circulates globally. This transformation bypasses traditional fact-checking systems and gives rise to new challenges as individuals can now publish content without oversight. The rapid dissemination of unverified information on these platforms has not only blurred the lines between truth and falsehood but also reshaped the public discourse landscape. As algorithms prioritize engagement over accuracy, the resulting echo chambers trap users within their existing belief systems, further complicating truth discernment. Influencer culture adds another layer to this issue, as personal views often intermingle with factual reporting, creating confusion about what should be trusted. This widespread diffusion of misleading narratives, especially those crossing geographical boundaries, poses significant threats to democracies around the world.

The chapter delves into various facets of social media's role in disinformation. It begins by examining the evolution of social media platforms and their impact on information sharing, highlighting how and why it has become challenging to filter out falsehoods from verified facts. The discussion progresses to explore how algorithms drive engagement and the consequences of prioritizing sensationalism at the expense of accurate content. Emphasis is placed on understanding how these digital mechanisms contribute to perceived polarization and the entrenchment of misinformation within society. Additionally, the chapter scrutinizes the complexities introduced by influencer culture and globalization, both of which exacerbate the spread of misleading narratives. The concluding segments focus on potential regulatory measures and policy interventions aimed at increasing transparency and accountability among tech companies, ensuring that democratic processes remain robust in the face of digital misinformation. Through this expository examination, the chapter seeks to provide insight into the ongoing challenges posed by social media in the realm of democratic integrity.

## Evolution of Social Media Platforms

Social media platforms have profoundly influenced how information is shared, often bypassing traditional fact-checking systems. This shift has reshaped public discourse in significant ways. In the past, news agencies upheld standards that ensured a level of accuracy and accountability. Today, social media allows anyone to publish information. The rapid spread of content can make it difficult to distinguish between verified facts and falsehoods. According to Schleffer & Miller (2021), the phenomenon of "fake news" on these platforms illustrates this challenge, as information designed to mislead users gains traction without being scrutinized by any editorial oversight.

The role of algorithms in driving engagement further exacerbates this issue. These complex algorithms are designed to capture user attention through personalized content recommendations based on previous interactions. Social media thrives on engagement; thus, posts and articles that provoke emotional reactions tend to be prioritized. As noted by Woodruff & Seitchik (2024), such algorithms cultivate echo chambers where only similar viewpoints are amplified, reinforcing existing biases and stifling meaningful dialogue across differing perspectives. Users are repeatedly exposed to content that supports their beliefs, making them less receptive to opposing views.

Influencer culture also plays a pivotal role in shaping perceptions and complicating truth discernment. Influencers often possess authority over vast audiences who regard their opinions as credible sources of information. Yet, influencers frequently blend personal views with factual reporting, blurring lines between what is opinion and what is grounded in evidence. This mixing muddles the clarity needed for informed decision-making, especially when influencer content swiftly goes viral.

The impact of globalization cannot be underestimated. Social media knows no borders, enabling disinformation to cross regions with unprecedented speed and reach. Instances are plentiful where misleading narratives—originating from foreign entities—have manipulated public perception during critical democratic events like elections. Authoritarian and illiberal regimes skillfully utilize these tools to disseminate propaganda and misinformation beyond their countries' confines, a trend highlighted by Schleffer & Miller (2021). Such practices threaten the integrity of electoral processes worldwide, demonstrating how easily false information can incite instability.

Moreover, the democratizing potential of social media is increasingly overshadowed by its capacity to serve political agendas. While it gives voice to grassroots movements and marginalized communities, it equally offers a platform for extremist ideologies, thereby escalating tensions within societies already polarized along ideological lines.

## Algorithmic Influences on Information Dissemination

In the digital landscape, algorithms are pivotal in determining the information flow on social media, prioritizing user engagement over the accuracy of content. By optimizing for sensationalism, these algorithms often amplify misinformation, underscoring emotionally charged narratives that entice more clicks and shares. This process not only fuels the spread of falsehoods but also manipulates public perception by highlighting extreme and polarizing content. Studies show how algorithms contribute to perceived polarization, making extremist opinions more visible while obscuring moderate voices (Bail, 2021). This emphasis on sensationalism can distort reality, creating a fertile ground for misinformation to flourish unchecked.

Additionally, filter bubbles instigated by algorithmic sorting mechanisms further exacerbate the situation. Users are exposed to content that aligns with their existing beliefs, shielding them from diverse viewpoints and reinforcing their biases. These echo chambers stagnate debate and diminish opportunities for critical discourse, as they create an environment where only homogenized opinions thrive. This phenomenon leads to a fragmented online community, divided by differing realities shaped by personalized information feeds. As a result, individuals become increasingly detached from opposing views, complicating efforts toward constructive dialogue or compromise.

Tech companies face significant criticism for placing profit over the integrity of information shared on their platforms. Their business models heavily depend on maximizing user engagement, often at the expense of factuality and reliability. The monetization of attention drives these platforms to promote content that keeps users hooked, regardless of its truthfulness or societal impact (The Algorithmic Management of Polarization and Violence on Social Media, n.d.). While this approach benefits companies financially, it raises ethical concerns about their responsibility to ensure the dissemination of accurate information. Critics argue that transparency in algorithmic processes is crucial for maintaining democratic communication and preventing misinformation from unduly influencing public opinion.

To address these challenges, policy interventions are imperative. Regulatory measures that enforce algorithmic transparency can play a vital role in safeguarding democratic systems against the proliferation of disinformation. By mandating greater openness regarding the criteria used to prioritize content, policymakers can hold tech companies accountable for the data shaping public discourse. Such interventions would require platforms to disclose their algorithms' decision-making processes, allowing users to understand how content is filtered and ranked. This transparency could lead to more informed media consumption and reduced susceptibility to manipulation by misleading content.

Moreover, policy solutions could incentivize platform redesigns that mitigate harmful effects of current algorithmic priorities. For instance, encouraging the development of algorithms that elevate nuanced discussions over polarizing rhetoric might foster healthier online conversations. Governments and civil society organizations could collaborate to establish standards that prioritize high-quality information and discourage the propagation of divisive content. Implementing such frameworks poses challenges, particularly in navigating the balance between regulation and free speech. Nonetheless, these efforts are essential for cultivating an online ecosystem conducive to democratic engagement and resilient against the tide of misinformation.

Despite these proposed measures, the road to meaningful change remains fraught with obstacles. Tech companies have shown resistance to altering their profitable models, often engaging in superficial adjustments rather than substantive reforms. Additionally, the rapid evolution of digital media poses difficulties in designing adaptable regulations that keep pace with emerging technologies. However, the stakes are too high to permit inaction. Platforms must acknowledge their role in shaping public consciousness and take proactive steps to counter disinformation effectively. Raising awareness about algorithmic influences and fostering critical media literacy among users are equally important components of any comprehensive strategy to combat misinformation.

## Effects on Public Perception

In the digital age, social media platforms have become fertile ground for the spread of disinformation, profoundly influencing public opinion and challenging democratic processes. The repetitive nature of exposure to falsehoods plays a critical role in shaping beliefs by creating an "illusion of truth." This psychological phenomenon makes it increasingly difficult for individuals to differentiate between fact and fiction, thereby weakening trust in established credible sources (Ognyanova et al., 2020). As people encounter the same misinformation repeatedly through shares, likes, and algorithmically driven content, the false information gains a veneer of credibility simply due to its persistent presence across their newsfeeds.

A poignant example can be derived from the 2020 U.S. elections, where misinformation circulated widely across multiple platforms. Case studies have shown how manipulated narratives about voter fraud and election integrity gained traction, causing confusion and skepticism among voters. Misinformation affected informed decision-making, as seen when certain counties refused to certify election results due to baseless concerns about voting machines, leading to legal interventions for resolution (Sanchez & Middlemass, 2022).

Fortunately, several initiatives are working toward countering this trend by reinforcing public knowledge and awareness. Fact-checkers and information literacy programs play pivotal roles in enhancing the ability of the populace to discern factual information from false data. Media literacy courses, required in states like Illinois and now incorporated in Colorado schools, provide young people with tools to critically assess the information they consume online. These programs aim to equip the next generation with skills necessary to navigate an increasingly complex media landscape, thereby fostering resilience against misinformation.

Moreover, various states have instituted proactive measures aimed at myth-busting and combating disinformation. For example, New Mexico's Secretary of State developed an election-specific fact-checking website, while North Carolina's "Mythbuster Monday" initiative targets voting myths via social media outreach. By rooting out early misinformation narratives, such efforts aim to prevent falsehoods from gaining momentum and becoming deeply entrenched in public belief systems.

Combating well-entrenched narratives, however, requires comprehensive educational efforts that address the motivations underlying people's beliefs in misinformation. Individuals often cling to false narratives because these stories resonate with existing biases or reinforce ideological preferences. To effectively challenge these ingrained beliefs, multifaceted approaches that engage individuals on a community level are necessary. Initiatives involving community leaders and trusted figures leveraging established relationships within religious institutions and community-based organizations have been identified as ways to engage individuals in meaningful dialogues.

Creating spaces where facts can be presented by those whom communities respect allows for more impactful persuasion, ultimately correcting misconceptions over time. While these efforts require significant investment and are unlikely to yield immediate results, they serve the long-term goal of reducing the prevalence and impact of misinformation on democratic societies.

Implementing rapid response strategies further supports this battle against misinformation. Colorado's establishment of Rapid Response Election Security Cyber Units exemplifies how localized cyber defense mechanisms can actively monitor and mitigate the spread of falsehoods related to election procedures. By employing dedicated teams to identify and disable accounts that perpetuate misinformation, alongside collaboration with major social media companies to enforce stricter content policies, a defensive infrastructure is created to protect the integrity of electoral processes.

However, the effectiveness of these actions hinges on sustained commitment and strategic coordination across local, state, and national levels. Social media corporations hold considerable power and responsibility in curtailing misinformation, and their cooperation is crucial. Policy interventions can facilitate this collaboration by mandating greater transparency and accountability within tech companies, ensuring that profit motives do not overshadow the necessity for preserving information integrity.

## Strategies to Combat Disinformation

Amid rising concerns about the spread of disinformation and its impact on democracy, individuals and organizations have a crucial role to play in countering these threats. The first step towards combating disinformation is promoting media literacy. Media literacy empowers people to critically evaluate and question the information they encounter daily. It enables individuals to discern credible sources from false narratives, thereby fostering resilience against misinformation.

To cultivate media literacy, it is important to introduce educational programs that engage communities in learning about different aspects of media consumption. These programs should encompass tools and techniques for analyzing digital content while understanding authorship, context, and intent. As reported by the Pew Research Center, with 26% of U.S. adults getting their news from YouTube—often from independent channels spreading conspiracies—it becomes increasingly vital to foster critical thinking skills among media consumers (Staff, n.d.). This approach maximizes the individual's ability to navigate complex information landscapes, ensuring they remain informed without falling victim to disinformation traps.

Technology also plays a pivotal role in identifying and flagging disinformation. Nevertheless, reliance solely on technological solutions presents limitations due to issues such as finite resources, legal authority, and civic trust (*Countering Disinformation Effectively: An Evidence-Based Policy Guide*, n.d.). To tackle these constraints, a diversified strategy involving technology can enhance fact-checking efficacy. Algorithms are employed to detect patterns consistent with fake news production, helping users recognize problematic content before dissemination. Platforms like Facebook and Twitter have implemented measures that label misleading posts, enabling users to make informed decisions about what they read or share. However, this approach requires continual reassessment for success, as technological innovations alone cannot guarantee a complete shield against disinformation.

Community-based initiatives offer another effective strategy. By engaging diverse populations in dialogues about truthfulness and reliability, these initiatives promote accurate communication. Local journalists, educators, and civic leaders work collaboratively to build networks that serve as reliable sources of information. These efforts emphasize the importance of direct engagement within communities to strengthen public discourse and empower citizens with trustworthy data. Supporting local journalism has shown potential to reduce disinformation, although financial sustainability remains a challenge requiring creative solutions such as philanthropy or government intervention (*Countering Disinformation Effectively: An Evidence-Based Policy Guide*, n.d.).

Lastly, proactive communication emphasizes using transparent and verified sources. Institutions and governments must engage with communities openly, providing verifiable information that counters inaccurate narratives. The responsibility extends beyond simply offering facts; it involves actively correcting false claims and participating in honest dialogues to restore trust. Public campaigns backed by rigorous evidence can act as powerful tools to counter disinformation, leveraging storytelling and emotional appeals that connect with audiences on a personal level.

Engaging in reflective practices is essential for individuals as well. Encouraging self-reflection when consuming media messages helps in evaluating the credibility and bias present in content. The SIFT Method, which stands for Stop, Investigate the source, Find better coverage, and Trace claims to the original context, can be utilized to systematically assess media credibility (Staff, n.d.). By questioning the intention behind messages, who benefits, and who might be harmed, individuals gain a deeper understanding of media influence.

## Regulatory Challenges and Solutions

The regulatory landscape in social media has increasingly become a battleground as societies struggle to balance the ideals of freedom of speech with the urgent need to counter disinformation. Current frameworks, devised in earlier times when traditional media dominated, are unfortunately lagging behind the rapid evolution of digital platforms. This gap leaves modern societies vulnerable to harmful content, necessitating policy reform to keep pace with technological advancements.

Many existing regulatory measures inadequately address the complexities introduced by digital media's multifaceted nature. In an era where information spreads at lightning speed and often without verification, outdated rules fail to tackle the nuanced ways in which disinformation disseminates and influences public discourse and democratic integrity. Reform in this area is critical not only to catch up with these advancements but also to mitigate the real-world consequences that arise when false information proliferates unchecked. Early steps could involve tailoring regulations that specifically target how content is managed across various platforms, considering the distinct modalities of each.

Potentially effective regulation models emerge through international cooperation and evidence-based approaches. Disinformation knows no geographic boundaries, spreading swiftly beyond the control of any single nation. Thus, collaborative international efforts are necessary to craft policies that transcend national lines and offer a unified response to disinformation challenges. Such cooperation can be seen in agreements where countries work together to establish norms that ensure responsible behavior across borders and align with democratic values.

Evidence-based policymaking stands crucial in this regard, providing a foundation upon which regulatory strategies can be built. By drawing insights from comprehensive studies and ongoing research into disinformation dynamics, policymakers can form responses grounded in empirical data. For instance, implementing systems that require transparency in platform algorithms and content moderation practices can help uncover biases that contribute to misinformation spread, thereby enhancing accountability.

Stakeholders play an essential role in developing and implementing these best practices. Platforms, governments, non-governmental organizations, and academic institutions must collaborate to foster responsible behavior among digital service providers. This collaboration enables the creation of standards that promote transparency, authenticity, and accuracy in shared information. Moreover, multilateral dialogues engaging diverse stakeholders can pave the way for innovation in tackling disinformation while safeguarding free expression.

One approach posited involves establishing guidelines for content validity and instituting verification mechanisms to ensure information integrity. Another suggestion includes incentivizing platforms to adopt practices that prioritize truthfulness, such as improved fact-checking procedures and enhanced user reporting tools. However, achieving consensus on these initiatives requires a commitment from all parties involved to uphold ethical standards and support initiatives that combat disinformation effectively.

As we look towards the future, it's evident that new challenges will continue to arise, demanding agile responses from regulators. Emerging technologies, including artificial intelligence and deepfake software, threaten to further complicate efforts to combat disinformation. These technologies can create hyper-realistic fabricated content capable of deceiving even the most discerning individuals, presenting novel risks to democracy and informed citizenry.

Anticipating these developments demands foresight from policymakers to stay ahead of potential threats. Regulatory bodies must engage in continuous learning, adapting their methods as trends evolve and conducting impact assessments of emerging technologies. They should also invest in research communities equipped to explore the implications of cutting-edge tools and develop strategies to counteract resulting disinformation threats.

Moreover, some argue for a diversified policy portfolio that embraces both short-term actions and long-term structural reforms. While interventions like immediate content labeling or takedown requests offer quick fixes, they might not address the underlying issues fueling disinformation spread. Long-term solutions, such as bolstering media literacy education and supporting local journalism, prove vital in fostering a well-informed populace less susceptible to misleading narratives (*Countering Disinformation Effectively: An Evidence-Based Policy Guide*, n.d.).

Governments might consider offering support to independent media outlets engaged in fact-checking and investigative journalism, ensuring such assistance is delivered through neutral frameworks to prevent political bias (*Digital Governance: Disinformation and Information Integrity - Open Government Partnership*, 2024). Public financing options should be transparent and involve regular audits to maintain credibility and trust in this aspect of governance.

Efforts to regulate disinformation need to remain flexible to accommodate varying national contexts and cultural nuances. What works in one region may not translate effectively elsewhere, given differences in societal structures, media landscapes, and political climates. Nevertheless, by maintaining open lines of communication and sharing successful tactics across jurisdictions, nations can collectively enhance their resilience against disinformation.

# Concluding Thoughts

This chapter has explored how social media platforms contribute to the spread of disinformation and its impact on democratic processes. By examining the unfiltered sharing of information, the role of algorithms, and the rise of influencer culture, it reveals a landscape where truth often takes a back seat to engagement and profit. The unchecked proliferation of false narratives fosters echo chambers, fueling polarization and undermining public trust in credible sources. Such dynamics complicate efforts to maintain informed citizenry vital for healthy democracies.

While various strategies attempt to counter these challenges, the path forward remains daunting. Efforts from fact-checking initiatives to regulatory policy proposals highlight the complexity of aligning digital media practices with democratic values, but significant barriers persist. Technological advancements outpace regulatory measures, while tech companies show reluctance toward meaningful change. Addressing disinformation requires sustained commitment across local, national, and global scales, demanding adaptive responses amidst evolving digital landscapes. In this uncertain environment, ongoing vigilance and innovation become essential tools in safeguarding the integrity of democratic discourse.

# Reference List

*Countering Disinformation Effectively: An Evidence-Based Policy Guide.* (n.d.). Carnegieendowment.org. https://carnegieendowment.org/research/2024/01/countering-disinformation-effectively-an-evidence-based-policy-guide

*Digital Governance: Disinformation and Information Integrity - Open Government Partnership.* (2024, October 11). Open Government Partnership. https://www.opengovpartnership.org/open-gov-guide/digital-governanc

e-disinformation-and-information-integrity/

Metzler, H., & Garcia, D. (2023, July 19). *Social Drivers and Algorithmic Mechanisms on Digital Media.* Perspectives on Psychological Science; SAGE Publishing. https://doi.org/10.1177/17456916231185057

Ognyanova, K., Lazer, D., Robertson, R. E., & Wilson, C. (2020, June 2). *Misinformation in action: Fake news exposure is linked to lower trust in media, higher trust in government when your side is in power.* Harvard Kennedy School Misinformation Review. https://doi.org/10.37016/mr-2020-024

Staff, R. (n.d.). *A media literacy expert shares 3 tips to dodge disinformation.* UAB Reporter. https://www.uab.edu/reporter/resources/learning-development/item/10133-a-media-literacy-expert-shares-3-tips-to-dodge-disinformation

Sanchez, G., & Middlemass, K. (2022, July 26). *Misinformation is eroding the public's confidence in democracy.* Brookings; The Brookings Institution. https://www.brookings.edu/articles/misinformation-is-eroding-the-publics-confidence-in-democracy/

Schleffer, G., & Miller, B. (2021). *The Political Effects of Social Media Platforms on Different Regime Types.* Texas National Security Review. https://tnsr.org/2021/07/the-political-effects-of-social-media-platforms-on-different-regime-types/

*The Algorithmic Management of Polarization and Violence on Social Media.* (n.d.).

Knightcolumbia.org. https://knightcolumbia.org/content/the-algorithmic-management-of-polarization-and-violence-on-social-media


Woodruff, J., & Seitchik, C. (2024, September 11). *Social media's role in fueling extremism and misinformation in a divided political climate.* PBS News; PBS News. https://www.pbs.org/newshour/show/social-medias-role-in-fueling-extremism-and-misinformation-in-a-divided-political-climate

# Tensions Between Enlightenment Values and Religious Faith

Examining the tensions between Enlightenment values and religious faith reveals a complex and often fraught relationship. The chapter delves into how these two cornerstone beliefs intersected in history, affecting the development of democratic principles. By investigating the Enlightenment's push toward reason and individual rights, contrasted against the deep-seated grip of religious traditions, one can understand the clashes that occurred as society attempted to balance rational governance with spiritual heritage. This dynamic imbalance often resulted in a challenging coexistence, which has long been a source of philosophical and practical debate.

The chapter explores various historical scenarios where the friction between these ideologies was most pronounced, notably during significant cultural shifts like the French and American Revolutions. These periods of upheaval highlight how Enlightenment ideals called for freedom and equality, sometimes directly opposing religious authority. The narrative further traces how this ongoing tension influenced the formation of modern democratic systems, shaping constitutional frameworks that sought to accommodate both rational secularism and religious pluralism. Readers are guided through pivotal debates, illuminating the challenges and complexities of integrating diverse perspectives within a democratic framework, while underscoring the enduring impact of this ideological conflict on contemporary societal issues.

## Historical Interactions Between Faith and Reason

The Age of Enlightenment, spanning roughly from the late 17th to the 19th century, marked an intellectual watershed in Europe that shifted the axis from tradition and religious orthodoxy towards reason and empirical evidence. This period emphasized individualism, human rights, and scientific inquiry, challenging the prevailing religious institutions and dogmas that had dominated European life. As such, the Enlightenment played a crucial role in shaping modern democratic principles by questioning established authority and advocating for rational governance.

Central to the Enlightenment was the belief that reason should be the primary guide in human affairs. Philosophers like Voltaire, Montesquieu, and Rousseau critiqued the traditional power structures and religious doctrines, arguing instead for systems based on logic and universal principles. Montesquieu's "Spirit of Laws" (1748) advocated for a separation of powers within government as a means of preventing tyranny, a concept which later became foundational in many democratic constitutions, including those in America and France. These ideas directly challenged the divine right of kings and the entrenched authority of the Church, proposing instead that governments derive their legitimacy from the will of the governed and the protection of their rights. Such notions of governance underpinned the philosophical undercurrents of the American and French Revolutions, wherein Enlightenment ideals greatly influenced democratic development. (The Enlightenment and Human Rights, n.d.)

However, this shift towards reason did not occur without resistance or adaptation within religious circles. Some religious figures sought to harmonize faith with reason, viewing these changing times as opportunities to re-interpret theological teachings in light of new knowledge. John Locke, for example, despite his emphasis on natural rights and reason, saw no conflict between faith and the functions of government, advocating for religious tolerance. Conversely, there were staunch defenders of religious orthodoxy who perceived Enlightenment thinking as a threat to spiritual authority and societal morality. This tension created vivid debates over the role of religion in public life and its influence on social reform.

One prominent instance where these tensions erupted into conflict was during the French Revolution. The revolution was fueled by Enlightenment principles urging liberty, equality, and fraternity, against a backdrop of sociopolitical oppression and economic hardship. Revolutionary leaders saw the Catholic Church as complicit in upholding the ancien régime's unjust hierarchy. Consequently, the French Revolution witnessed significant anti-clerical movements aimed at reducing religious influence in state affairs, often leading to violence and the forced secularization of society. Despite the turmoil, these events illustrated the complex interactions between faith and reason, highlighting the challenges of integrating them within a single governing framework (Bristow, 2010).

These historic confrontations and collaborations fundamentally affected how constitutional frameworks developed over time. The French Declaration of the Rights of Man and Citizen (1789), inspired by Enlightenment thought, espoused secular values yet aimed to maintain religious freedoms. Similarly, the American Constitution enshrined principles of religious liberty and church-state separation, ensuring that faith could coexist with rational, secular governance. Both documents exemplified attempts to balance individual freedoms, including religious expression, with rational lawmaking practices.

Moreover, as newly independent nations crafted their laws, they faced the difficult task of incorporating diverse perspectives, including those shaped by religious values and Enlightenment philosophies. This endeavor required nuanced understanding and compromise, ensuring that various faiths could contribute to moral discourse while allowing reason to inform policy and governance. The result was the creation of systems that respected both individual choice in religious belief and the necessity of a neutral state role in matters of conscience.

## Impact on American Democratic Development

The formation of American democracy was significantly influenced by the tensions between Enlightenment values and religious beliefs. The Founding Fathers faced a monumental task in deciding whether to separate church and state or to root their governance in a moral framework inspired by religion. This debate is emblematic of the broader tension between reason, heralded by Enlightenment thinkers, and faith, which was deeply embedded in the fabric of society at the time.

The Founding Fathers were products of the Enlightenment, an era that emphasized reason, skepticism of authority, and empirical evidence over tradition. This intellectual movement inspired ideas about individual liberty and democratic self-governance. However, many of these leaders also acknowledged the potential for religion to provide a moral compass, which they believed was necessary for fostering civic virtue among citizens. For instance, while Thomas Jefferson fiercely advocated for the separation of church and state to prevent government interference in religious matters, he also recognized the moral teachings of religion as beneficial for society (Rosen, 2022).

This philosophical balancing act came to a head in the drafting of the First Amendment, which guarantees religious freedom and reflects Enlightenment influences. James Madison, often hailed as the architect of the Constitution, argued cogently for this amendment, advocating for the "free exercise" of religion rather than mere toleration (American Experience, 2019). This approach allowed for diverse religious expression and ensured that government could not impose any single religious ideology on its citizens. By embedding these principles into the nation's foundational legal document, the framers created a space for both religious pluralism and secular governance—an embodiment of Enlightenment ideals.

As America evolved, ongoing cultural conflicts surfaced, revealing the underlying tensions between reason and faith in modern social issues. These conflicts are vivid in debates over educational curricula, reproductive rights, and LGBTQ+ rights, where reasoning informed by scientific understanding often clashes with traditional religious beliefs. Such debates expose the enduring struggle to balance rational thought with faith-based perspectives in public policy-making.

Moreover, entrenched philosophical questions about moral authority persist in challenging representation and policymaking. Questions such as who holds moral authority—reason or faith—remain central to discussions about lawmaking and governance. For instance, debates around issues like climate change and healthcare reflect tensions between empirical data-driven policies and religiously motivated positions that emphasize stewardship of creation and compassion for the needy. These enduring philosophical dilemmas continue to inform political discourse, impacting how laws represent various belief systems within a pluralistic democracy.

## Generational Perspectives on Liberty and Faith

Examining the perceptions of different generations towards liberty and religious beliefs reveals significant insights into how democracy has been shaped over the decades. Each generational cohort brings a unique set of values and experiences that influence their view of this relationship, thus contributing to ongoing societal discussions.

Baby Boomers, born between 1946 and 1964, are often characterized by their role in pivotal movements, such as the civil rights movement. During the 1960s and 70s, they witnessed profound social changes and were instrumental in balancing Enlightenment values with traditional beliefs. As this generation sought equality and justice, they navigated the delicate balance between religious convictions and the universal values of freedom and equality espoused by democratic ideals. Notably, Baby Boomers were engaged in debates concerning church involvement in the state, advocating for policies that reflected both moral integrity and modern Enlightenment thinking. Their activism showcased a commitment to harmonizing evolving societal norms with rooted spiritual beliefs, highlighting their ability to maintain traditional morals while embracing aspects of reform crucial to advancing civil rights (Parker et al., 2019).

Generation X, following the Baby Boomers and born between 1965 and 1980, faced an era defined by economic uncertainty and political cynicism. Growing up during times of recession and witnessing institutional failures, Generation X developed a skepticism toward established systems, including religious organizations. This skepticism fostered a strong emphasis on individualism, a hallmark of their ideological stance. For many Generation Xers, the notion of liberty became intertwined not just with freedom from oppression but with the autonomy to question authority and carve personal paths independent of rigid structures. Their ethos represented a departure from the collective activism of the previous generation, focusing instead on self-discovery and the diverse ways individuals could manifest religious beliefs, detached from institutional dogma (PRRI, 2024).

In contrast, Millennials (born 1981-1996) and Generation Z (born 1997-2012) have come of age in an era where inclusivity and diversity take precedence. These younger generations prioritize inclusivity, questioning traditional morals and often championing secularism. With the rise of digital communication, these cohorts are more exposed to diverse worldviews that challenge conventional religious narratives. As such, they actively engage in discussions about secularism versus traditional values, often advocating for spaces that respect various identities and belief systems. The shift reflects a broader move towards acceptance and understanding, which they see as integral to fostering liberty within a democratic framework. Millennials and Gen Z encounter the Enlightenment's legacy through their advocacy for equality and critique of exclusionary practices, propelling debates surrounding the redefinition of morality in public life (Parker et al., 2019).

These generational perspectives feed into broader societal activism, revealing clear divides yet also opportunities for bridging gaps. Activism across generations demonstrates varying interpretations of faith and democratic values, illustrating how each cohort engages with religion and liberty within a political context. While Baby Boomers might draw from religious teachings to inform their activism, younger generations may focus on ethical principles derived from humanistic philosophies, seeking solutions that transcend traditional religious frameworks. The generational divide in activism underscores the evolving nature of the discourse around democracy and religious freedom, posing questions about how these differing viewpoints can coexist and be reconciled in contemporary society.

Evidence of this divide is seen in how each generation responds to pressing issues like climate change, racial justice, and gender equality—topics where religious beliefs and liberties often intersect. Baby Boomers may approach these challenges by integrating biblical stewardship or compassion, whereas Millennials and Gen Z may discuss environmental ethics through the lens of social responsibility devoid of religious connotations. In contrast, Generation X might navigate these complexities by prioritizing personal freedoms and carefully considering the interplay between individual rights and collective wellbeing. The diversity in approaches provides a nuanced understanding of liberty vis-à-vis religious faith, reflecting the complex tapestry of American democratic values.

Understanding these varied generational perceptions is crucial for politically engaged individuals and academics alike in navigating current democratic challenges. By examining how diverse groups articulate their visions of liberty and interpret religious beliefs, it becomes possible to identify areas of consensus and discord. This understanding is essential for developing inclusive policies that honor the pluralistic nature of contemporary democracy while respecting the historical threads that have woven together faith and freedom.

## Role of Education in Bridging Differences

Education stands as a potent tool capable of bridging the divide between Enlightenment values and religious beliefs. While these two forces have historically been posed as dichotomous—rational thought versus faith—they can be harmoniously integrated through educational frameworks. At the heart of this reconciliation lies curriculum design that emphasizes critical thinking and comparative religion.

The modern curricula in schools are being increasingly designed to introduce students to diverse worldviews, fostering an environment where reason and faith coexist. By presenting information on various belief systems in parallel, educators promote not merely tolerance but a deeper understanding of religious perspectives. Critical thinking is encouraged by challenging students to interrogate their assumptions, examine contradictory viewpoints, and appreciate the complexity inherent in both secular and religious narratives. This approach aligns with Prothero's perspective on religious literacy, which suggests that understanding different religious traditions is essential for effective citizenship (Prothero, 2007). The inclusion of such curricular elements is crucial for nurturing a generation adept at navigating complex social landscapes marked by diversity and polarizing beliefs.

Higher education institutions play a pivotal role in mediating the dialogue between Enlightenment ideals and religious faith. Universities serve as arenas where debates about faith and reason are actively pursued, fostering intellectual growth and interfaith collaboration. For instance, many universities incorporate courses that directly tackle the reconciliation of conflicting ideologies through philosophical dilemmas or historical case studies. Such engagement allows students to experience firsthand the interplay of rationality and spirituality, providing them a broader lens through which to view human progress. Furthermore, these academic discussions often extend beyond the classroom, sparking collaborations between secular and religious student organizations. Through joint initiatives and community service projects, students develop an appreciation for the mutual benefits of combined efforts towards common goals (Moyaert, 2018).

Apart from formal education settings, community engagement plays a vital role in promoting dialogue between religious and secular groups. Community initiatives centered around shared stories and experiences create platforms for interaction where both sides can learn from each other. Interfaith dialogues often feature narratives that showcase shared human values, reinforced through collective memories of peace-building and overcoming adversity. This methodology echoes the findings of the European Commission-funded REDCo project, which highlighted the potential of educational environments as safe spaces for discussing religious and non-religious diversity (Jackson, 2011). These community programs foster respect and empathy, demonstrating that religious beliefs and secular values need not be adversaries; rather, they can function synergistically to uphold democratic principles.

Nonetheless, political polarization presents significant challenges to these educational efforts. As political ideologies become more entrenched, the task of creating inclusive educational environments becomes increasingly daunting. In several democracies across the world, this polarization has seeped into educational discourse, turning schools into battlegrounds for ideological supremacy. Educational policies must therefore evolve, prioritizing the inclusion of diverse narratives that bridge gaps and reduce hostility. This necessitates robust teacher training programs tailored to equip educators with skills necessary for handling sensitive discussions around faith and secularity, ensuring all voices are respected and valued.

Amidst this tension, it remains imperative for educational systems to champion inclusivity without compromising on academic rigor or moral pluralism. To achieve this, educational frameworks should integrate guidelines that encourage open-dialogue models, focusing on conflict resolution and appreciation of differences. Additionally, pedagogical methods should be refined to embrace varied learning styles, guaranteeing that students from all backgrounds find resonance in the material taught. Implementing practices such as peer-led workshops, multicultural events, and interdisciplinary seminars would facilitate a culture of mutual respect while reinforcing democratic ideals.

## Potential for Coexistence and Collaboration

In the realm of democracy, a harmonious coexistence between faith and reason remains essential. Historical instances showcase how religious organizations and secular groups can unite for social justice, illustrating this potential collaboration. A notable example is the civil rights movement in the United States during the 1950s and 1960s. Religious leaders, such as Martin Luther King Jr., worked alongside secular activists, highlighting the role that churches played in advocating for equal rights. These alliances not only advanced the civil rights agenda but also emphasized the power of combined efforts, where shared values transcended individual belief systems.

Interfaith dialogues represent another vital channel for bridging gaps between divergent beliefs. These discussions focus on common ethical concerns, fostering understanding and tolerance among different religious communities. For instance, interfaith initiatives led by the World Council of Churches have successfully brought together diverse religious denominations to address issues like poverty and environmental conservation. Such efforts underline the importance of dialogue in creating a cohesive society by concentrating on shared humanitarian goals rather than divisive doctrines (Academy for Cultural Diplomacy, 2024).

The emergence of civic engagement models has further encouraged grassroots efforts to promote democratic participation across various belief systems. These models advocate for inclusive governance, ensuring that different perspectives are represented in the democratic process. An example is the establishment of community-based organizations that unite people from different backgrounds to engage in local decision-making. These initiatives empower individuals, regardless of their religious affiliations, to contribute actively to societal development. This inclusivity fosters a sense of belonging and mutual respect, forming a foundation for a vibrant and participatory democracy (Faith and Civic Life - the Policy Circle, 2024).

A vision for a collaborative future necessitates commitment to dialogue and respect. To achieve this, it is crucial to imagine a society where faith and reason coexist and enrich each other, enhancing public discourse. This vision requires open-mindedness and a willingness to engage with differing viewpoints constructively. As Yuval Levin posits in "A Time to Build," this involves recognizing the importance of healthy institutions in civil society, which can be realized through building networks of friendship and coordinated action. By embracing diversity as a strength, societies can navigate complexities collaboratively, drawing upon both religious wisdom and rational analysis to address pressing issues (Faith and Civic Life - the

Policy Circle, 2024).

Guidelines for fostering these collaborations highlight the necessity of historical awareness, interfaith initiatives, civic models, and envisioning shared futures. Historically successful collaborations demonstrate that collective action towards common goals yields positive outcomes. In interfaith dialogue initiatives, setting aside conversion agendas in favor of genuine exchange encourages mutual growth and understanding. Civic engagement models thrive on inclusivity, emphasizing participation from all societal sectors. Imagining a collaborative future requires dedicated spaces for dialogue, where respect and peaceful coexistence guide interactions.

To effectively nurture the coexistence of faith and reason, it is imperative to establish frameworks rooted in dialogue and inclusion. Educating about diverse religious practices alongside secular principles can dismantle stereotypes, paving the way for informed conversations. Community forums, universities, and media platforms play pivotal roles in facilitating these exchanges. Through storytelling and personal narratives, individuals gain insights into varied experiences, fostering empathy and reducing prejudice.

Moreover, integrating faith-based perspectives into public discourse need not undermine secular ideals. Rather, it enriches societal narratives by introducing moral considerations often overlooked in purely secular debates. For instance, engaging faith communities in policy discussions about economic justice or environmental stewardship can bring nuanced perspectives that challenge conventional approaches. This inclusion broadens the scope of discourse, ensuring comprehensive solutions to complex problems.

## Insights and Implications

The chapter has explored the enduring tension between Enlightenment ideals and religious beliefs within the framework of democracy, revealing a persistent struggle to find harmony between reason and faith. From the Age of Enlightenment through historical events such as the French and American Revolutions, these conflicting ideologies have shaped democratic development, illustrating the challenges faced in integrating rational governance with spiritual beliefs. By examining generational perspectives and educational influences, the chapter unveils how each generation has grappled with these tensions, reflecting on their impact on societal norms and political discourse. Although attempts have been made to reconcile these opposing forces throughout history, achieving true balance remains elusive and fraught with philosophical and moral complexity.

As we consider the implications for contemporary society, it becomes evident that these historical tensions continue to manifest in modern debates over policy and representation. Despite some progress in fostering coexistence through education and dialogue, deep-seated divisions persist, often fueled by cultural conflicts and polarized viewpoints. The challenge lies not only in acknowledging these differences but also in seeking common ground upon which to build more inclusive democratic frameworks. However, the path forward remains uncertain, as entrenched philosophical questions about authority and morality continue to pervade discussions about governance. Whether we can truly integrate faith with reason to create a harmonious democratic society is a question that remains unresolved, highlighting the difficulties that lie ahead.

# Reference List

American Experience. (2019, February 6). *People and Ideas: Early America's Formation*. Pbs.org; American Experience. https://www.pbs.org/godinamer ica/people/thomas-jefferson.html

Academy for Cultural Diplomacy. (2024). *Academy for Cultural Diplomacy.* Www.culturaldiplomacy.org. https://www.culturaldiplomacy.org/academ y/index.php?en_historical-examples

Bristow, W. (2010, August 20). *Enlightenment (Stanford Encyclopedia of*

*Philosophy)*. Stanford.edu; Stanford University. https://plato.stanford.edu/entries/enlightenment/

*Faith and Civic Life - The Policy Circle.* (2024, September 30). The Policy Circle. https://www.thepolicycircle.org/brief/faith-and-civic-life/

Jackson, R. (2011, March). *Religion, education, dialogue and conflict: editorial introduction.* British Journal of Religious Education. https://doi.org/10.1080/01416200.2011.545266

Moyaert, M. (2018, January). *On the Role of Ritual in Interfaith Education.* Religious Education. https://doi.org/10.1080/00344087.2017.1383869

PRRI. (2024, January 22). *A Political and Cultural Glimpse Into America's Future: Generation Z's Views on Generational Change and the Challenges and Opportunities Ahead | PRRI.* PRRI | at the Intersection of Religion, Values, and Public Life. https://www.prri.org/research/generation-zs-views-on-generational-change-and-the-challenges-and-opportunities-ahead-a-political-and-cultural-glimpse-into-americas-future/

Parker, K., Graf, N., & Igielnik, R. (2019, January 17). *Generation Z Looks a Lot Like Millennials on Key Social and Political Issues.* Pew Research Center. https://www.pewresearch.org/social-trends/2019/01/17/generation-z-looks-a-lot-like-millennials-on-key-social-and-political-issues/

Rosen, J. (2022). *From Jefferson to Brandeis: The First Amendment, the Declaration, and the Constitution | Constitution Center.* National Constitution

Center – Constitutioncenter.org. https://constitutioncenter.org/go/firsta
mendment


*The Enlightenment and Human Rights.* (n.d.). Revolution.chnm.org. https://re
volution.chnm.org/exhibits/show/liberty---equality---fraternity/enlighte
nment-and-human-rights

# The Crisis of Solidarity

The crisis of solidarity emerges when social cohesion in democratic societies weakens, threatening the very fabric that holds communities together. Amidst this breakdown, the sense of belonging, trust, and mutual support that citizens typically enjoy begins to unravel, leading to a fragmented social structure. This chapter delves into the stark consequences of such fragmentation, illustrating how the erosion of these communal bonds disrupts the smooth functioning of democracy. With diverse groups finding it increasingly difficult to coexist peacefully, the ensuing turmoil has profound implications for both governance and societal stability. As the unity that once celebrated diversity diminishes, the ability of a society to collaboratively navigate its challenges wanes, casting a shadow over its democratic aspirations.

In exploring this theme, the chapter examines several key dimensions affected by the fracture in social unity. It investigates how weakened social ties contribute to increased political polarization, which in turn exacerbates divisions and hampers effective governance. Furthermore, the analysis highlights the interplay between economic disparities and socio-cultural factors that deepen existing rifts within communities. Readers will find a critical examination of the role that external threats, such as political extremism, play in widening these divides. The chapter also addresses the implications for civic engagement and public trust in institutions, noting the potential for destabilization when citizens lose faith in their leaders and the system at large. Through this exploration, the chapter aims to provide insights into the pressing need to rebuild social cohesion as a foundation for a resilient and functional democracy.

## Defining Social Cohesion in Democratic Societies

In the realm of democratic societies, social cohesion represents the adhesive that connects diverse individuals within a political framework. At its heart, social cohesion fosters a sense of belonging and trust among citizens, thereby stitching together a collective identity crucial for governance. This concept is particularly significant in democracies because it creates a cooperative atmosphere amid diversity. In everyday interactions and shared objectives, social cohesion builds vital connections among citizens, promoting harmony and reducing friction in pluralistic societies.

One key aspect is the ability of social cohesion to lower tensions in diverse democracies. In societies marked by different cultural, ethnic, or ideological groups, disparities can often lead to discord if left unaddressed. High levels of social cohesion help mitigate these potential tensions by providing common ground where differences coexist peacefully. The resilience of a democracy is inherently linked to this stability. When citizens feel part of a larger community with shared values, they are more likely to support democratic institutions and processes, fostering an environment where democracy can thrive.

Historically, the connection between strong social ties and democratic stability has been evident. Societies with well-established networks of social bonds typically experience fewer disruptions or retreats from democratic norms. Historical analysis reveals that when citizens share robust social connections, they become more actively engaged in civic life, often standing against authoritarian shifts. For instance, during times of political upheaval or economic challenges, cohesive societies have demonstrated a remarkable capacity to uphold democratic principles and resist autocratic temptations.

The measurement of social cohesion also provides valuable insights into the health of democratic systems. Surveys assessing aspects such as trust among citizens, engagement in community activities, and faith in public institutions are telling indicators. These measures can highlight underlying weaknesses within a democracy, such as rising political extremism or diminishing civic engagement. When citizens start losing faith in their governing bodies or in each other, it often leads to increased polarization and fragmentation. Thus, surveys acting as diagnostic tools can alert policymakers to address these issues proactively.

Economic, socio-cultural, and political threats further complicate the landscape of social cohesion. Economic disparities, such as inequality or lack of access to essential services, sow seeds of division. Similarly, socio-cultural variables like national identity and shared values shape perceptions within and among groups, while political polarization exacerbates existing divides. These threats are compounded when governments fail to recognize and manage them effectively, leading to weakened trust and reduced cohesion.

Given these challenges, defining social cohesion precisely remains tricky, as noted by organizations such as the United Nations Economic Commission for Europe (UNECE). The concept's broad nature allows for comprehensive analysis but may sometimes cloud the identification of specific issues. Nonetheless, understanding social cohesion's multi-dimensional nature supports efforts to enhance resilience across various societal domains.

The implications of social cohesion extend beyond mere conceptual debates; they touch on real-world governance outcomes. In a democracy, a cohesive society ensures that different voices contribute to a shared vision without dissolving into antagonistic factions. It nurtures a culture where diversity enriches rather than divides, encouraging constructive dialogue and inclusive policy-making. Such a society is better equipped to handle internal disagreements and external shocks, enhancing its long-term resilience.

## Consequences of Tribalism on Governance

Tribalism poses a significant threat to democratic governance by fostering an 'us vs. them' mentality, which corrodes civic relationships and hinders collaboration. This divisive mindset can be observed in various political landscapes where individuals gravitate towards groups that reflect their beliefs and values, often at the expense of broader societal cohesion. When people identify strongly with a particular group, they may view those outside their group as adversaries or threats. This dynamic fosters suspicion and hostility, and makes it difficult for diverse parties to engage in constructive dialogue and unite on shared goals.

The impact of tribal affiliations extends deeply into policy-making processes. Often, these affiliations prioritize party loyalty over the public interest. Politicians may push forward policies that align with their group's ideologies, even if those policies fail to address pressing societal issues effectively. The emphasis on maintaining a cohesive party line sometimes means that crucial problems are overlooked or inadequately addressed in favor of advancing partisan agendas. This approach not only neglects the needs of the populace but also erodes trust in leadership and government institutions (Calvert, 2020).

Furthermore, extreme partisanship, fueled by tribalism, contributes to legislative gridlock, thereby weakening democratic representation. In a system where compromise is essential for progress, entrenched partisan interests inhibit legislators from finding common ground. As each faction strives to dominate the political narrative, opportunities for meaningful collaboration diminish. This stalemate stalls legislative action and prevents the enactment of policies that could benefit society at large. Such gridlock leaves critical issues unresolved, depriving citizens of effective governance and exacerbating public disillusionment.

The frustration stemming from governance failures driven by tribal loyalties can lead to a dangerous cycle of disillusionment and increased support for extremist factions. Many citizens, feeling disenfranchised and overlooked, might resort to supporting radical movements that promise radical solutions to systemic problems. These movements capitalize on widespread dissatisfaction and exploit it to garner influence and power. As more people turn to extremism in search of reform, the imbalance between mainstream and fringe ideologies becomes pronounced, further polarizing the political landscape.

The corrosive effects of tribalism are illustrated in modern democracies worldwide. Political sectarianism—a form of tribalism—thrives when citizens perceive themselves primarily through politically charged identities. This perception transforms political opponents into irreconcilable foes whose ideologies pose existential threats. Instead of engaging with divergent views constructively, individuals seek solace within echo chambers where their biases remain unchallenged. This phenomenon amplifies division, making consensus nearly impossible.

Combatting the divisive nature of tribalism within democracies requires intentional efforts to bridge divides and promote understanding across different political affiliations. Encouraging open dialogues and fostering environments where diverse opinions can converge are vital steps toward dismantling the barriers erected by tribal instincts. By emphasizing shared human values over rigid ideological stances, societies can cultivate a culture of empathy and cooperation.

Moreover, policymakers must transcend narrow partisan interests to prioritize the greater good. Implementing inclusive practices that involve diverse voices in decision-making enriches policy outcomes and enhances democratic health. Engaging citizens holistically, rather than catering exclusively to specific constituencies, fosters trust in leadership and ensures equitable governance. Initiatives aimed at increasing transparency, accountability, and participation enhance democratic resilience against the detrimental effects of tribal entrenchment.

In education systems, promoting media literacy and critical thinking skills can equip individuals to navigate information landscapes saturated with bias and misinformation. Empowered citizens capable of analyzing diverse perspectives critically are less susceptible to manipulation by tribal narratives. Equipping people with tools to discern truth from propaganda is paramount in cultivating informed electorates who make decisions rooted in careful consideration rather than blind allegiance to party lines.

Ultimately, reversing the damaging course set by unchecked tribalism demands commitment from all sectors of society. Civic leaders, educators, media outlets, and citizens alike must collectively embrace strategies that emphasize unity, tolerance, and respect for divergent viewpoints. Building bridges where walls once stood involves challenging longstanding biases while steadfastly pursuing common goals that uplift communities. The antidote to division lies not only in highlighting differences but also in celebrating the rich tapestry of ideas that democracy thrives upon (Tijerina, 2020).

## Role of Civil Society in Maintaining Solidarity

Civil society organizations play an essential role in shaping democratic societies. Understanding this is crucial, especially as we navigate through periods where social cohesion is under threat. These organizations serve as a counterbalance to state power, promoting the health of democracy by fostering social capital and encouraging active participation from citizens. This involvement is not just about political engagement but is rooted in community-based activities that bring people together, bridging political divides and strengthening bonds through shared values.

In many democracies, civil society acts as a watchdog over governmental actions, keeping state power in check and holding officials accountable. When these organizations are vigilant, they expose corruption and advocate for transparency, creating an environment where democratic principles can flourish. The presence of civil society helps ensure state power is exercised responsibly, promoting good governance that aligns with the public's interests. They engage in lobbying for legislative reforms that restrict abuses of authority, helping to create systems where accountability is prized.

Community-based organizations are at the heart of civil society, engaging citizens in ways that strengthen social cohesion. They organize activities and forums that promote dialogue among diverse groups, encouraging understanding and cooperation across different social, cultural, and political spectrums. By doing so, they build trust and foster a sense of community amongst individuals who might otherwise remain isolated from each other due to political or ideological differences. These interactions lead to stronger societal networks, where individuals are more likely to support one another and work collaboratively towards common goals.

Initiatives by civil society also play a critical role in bridging divides between polarized political groups. In today's climate of heightened political tension, these organizations offer neutral spaces for dialogue and cooperation, facilitating conversations that help dissolve barriers and promote mutual understanding. By focusing on shared human values and common challenges, civil society initiatives encourage collaboration that transcends political affiliations. This approach not only assists in mending fractured relationships but also fosters a culture of peaceful coexistence and cooperative problem-solving.

Despite the influence of civil society, these organizations often face significant challenges, such as limited resources and outright hostility. Governments in some regions may attempt to curtail their activities, fearful of their power to mobilize and influence public opinion. Additionally, financial constraints can limit their ability to carry out programs effectively. However, even in the face of adversity, an active civil society continues to reinforce public faith in democratic institutions. Their persistence in advocating for rights and justice showcases their resilience and commitment to maintaining democratic norms.

The impact of civil society is evident in various contexts, including situations where democracy is fragile or emerging from authoritarian rule. In such cases, civil society becomes a beacon of hope, demonstrating how grassroots movements can instill democratic values and societal progress. For instance, as observed in Indonesia, civil society organizations (CSOs) actively participate in governmental processes by employing strategies like lobbying and public campaigns. They engage directly with policymakers to advocate for changes, striving to make government actions more transparent and accountable (Yudi Rusfiana & Dewi Kurniasih, 2024).

Beyond the immediate political sphere, civil society organizations contribute to the development of democratic cultures by educating citizens about their rights and responsibilities. They empower individuals to engage in dialogues, participate in elections, and advocate for changes within their communities. This educational aspect is vital, teaching tolerance and respect for opposing viewpoints—values that are indispensable for stable democracies.

Moreover, civil society acts as a platform for marginalized voices, offering an avenue for historically oppressed groups to assert their rights and interests. Through advocacy and lobbying, these groups can influence policy and promote inclusiveness, ensuring that democratic systems represent the diversity within societies. In doing so, civil society helps build a democracy that is not only representative but also equitable and just.

Finally, civil society organizations also provide a training ground for future leaders. By managing projects that address public issues, these organizations cultivate leadership skills and increase civic awareness among participants. This grassroots level of involvement ensures that future leaders emerge who understand the complexities of democratic citizenship and governance.

## Effects of Multiculturalism on Unity

In diverse democracies, multiculturalism plays a pivotal role in shaping social cohesion. At its core, multiculturalism acknowledges and respects the coexistence of multiple cultural identities within a single society. It underscores inclusivity by advocating for the integration of different ethnic, religious, and cultural groups into the democratic fabric. This concept not only celebrates diversity but also fosters an environment where citizens can engage harmoniously with one another, irrespective of their backgrounds.

First, multiculturalism serves as a catalyst for inclusivity and integration. By recognizing diverse identities, it facilitates participation and representation in democratic processes. Policies supporting multiculturalism encourage communities to embrace differences and appreciate their cultural heritage while interacting on common platforms that enhance understanding and cooperation. This approach mitigates risks associated with marginalization, thus promoting a more balanced and fair society.

Moreover, cultural diversity enriches democratic societies by introducing varied perspectives that drive innovation and empathy. When diverse cultures converge, they bring unique insights and solutions to complex societal issues, offering comprehensive policy alternatives tailored to address specific needs. For example, policies conceived through multicultural lenses often integrate suggestions that cater to a wider population, ensuring that minority voices are heard and respected. Empathy grows as individuals from different backgrounds learn from each other's experiences, fostering a sense of shared humanity and purpose.

However, the path to a cohesive society is fraught with challenges stemming from misunderstandings about cultural differences. In some instances, these misunderstandings can lead to social fragmentation, perpetuating stereotypes and breeding exclusionary practices. Addressing this requires evolving narratives that emphasize unity while respecting diversity. Encouraging dialogue and mutual respect among various cultural groups helps dismantle misconceptions, thereby reducing tensions and fostering a collective identity.

Successful integration strategies are essential in bridging gaps between differing cultural communities. Cross-cultural dialogue stands out as a powerful tool for promoting understanding and dispelling myths. Through open conversations, individuals gain insights into other cultures' values and traditions, facilitating acceptance and tolerance. Educational programs aimed at raising awareness and celebrating diversity also play a crucial role. By including multicultural education in curricula, societies equip younger generations with the skills needed to thrive in pluralistic environments, thereby embedding long-term cohesion.

Furthermore, aligning communities toward common goals strengthens bonds across cultural divides. Initiatives that focus on shared objectives, such as community development projects or environmental efforts, harness the strengths of diverse communities. These collaborations emphasize common interests and benefits, leading to increased solidarity and trust among participants. When communities unite around collective causes, they create a robust network of support that reinforces democratic values and enhances social cohesion.

## Strategies for Fostering Social Cohesion

The crisis of solidarity poses a profound threat to democratic functions, as societal divisions erode the very foundations of collective governance. In such times, actionable strategies to rebuild social cohesion are essential not only to stabilize communities but also to ensure the vitality and functionality of democratic systems. One key strategy involves fostering community engagement through local events and volunteer opportunities. These initiatives serve as a bridge, connecting individuals across diverse backgrounds to form a shared purpose. Local festivals, for instance, provide platforms for cultural exchange and mutual understanding, promoting an atmosphere where differences are celebrated rather than divisive.

Volunteer opportunities further amplify this sense of unity by bringing people together to tackle community issues, fostering an environment of cooperation. Such involvement not only addresses immediate needs but also cultivates long-term relationships and trust within communities. By participating in efforts like neighborhood clean-ups or food drives, citizens experience firsthand the benefits of teamwork and shared responsibility, driving home the idea that individual contributions are valuable components of a cohesive society.

Educational reforms stand as another crucial pillar in this endeavor. Focusing on civic values and media literacy is imperative to prepare citizens for informed participation in democratic processes. Education systems should aim to instill a deep understanding of civic duties and rights from an early age, ensuring that future voters are well-equipped to engage in thoughtful decision-making. Media literacy, in particular, empowers individuals to critically assess information, discern misinformation, and navigate digital spaces with confidence. This skill is vital in an era where digital disinformation can drastically sway public opinion and undermine democratic principles.

Moreover, political reforms targeting diverse representation and the inclusion of minority voices are integral to invigorating democratic governance. Diverse representation ensures that all segments of society have a seat at the table, contributing unique perspectives and solutions. Policies focused on equitable representation lead to more comprehensive and inclusive decision-making processes, which are reflective of the broader populace's interests and needs. Structural changes such as implementing proportional representation or eliminating barriers to candidacy for minority groups can significantly enhance fairness and equality in governance systems.

Furthermore, embracing technology as a tool for enhancing social cohesion presents both opportunities and challenges. When used effectively, technology fosters online connections and encourages respectful dialogues across communities. Social media platforms and digital forums can serve as modern town squares, where ideas and experiences are exchanged. However, this requires vigilant oversight to prevent the spread of hate speech and misinformation, which can fracture societal bonds. Therefore, establishing clear guidelines and ethical frameworks for online engagement is critical to maximizing technology's potential to build rather than disrupt.

To facilitate successful integration strategies, it's important to create environments that encourage participation from all communities. Providing resources and support for multicultural dialogue and interaction can help break down barriers and build bridges between different cultural groups. Educational programs focusing on shared history and common goals can foster unity and resilience against divisive narratives.

Strategically leveraging these educational, political, and technological reforms can reaffirm democratic values and strengthen governance structures. However, it's pivotal that these strategies are implemented in a manner sensitive to the unique characteristics and needs of each community. This targeted approach will ensure that initiatives are relevant and impactful, ultimately leading to a stronger, more cohesive society.

## Concluding Thoughts

This chapter has delved into the critical issue of how deteriorating social cohesion impacts democratic functions. It highlighted the ways in which a lack of unity and trust among citizens can destabilize the democratic process, often leading to increased polarization and inefficiencies in governance. When individuals feel alienated or disconnected from one another, support for democratic institutions wanes, and factions form based on narrow interests rather than shared values. The breakdown in social cohesion makes it difficult to address societal challenges collectively, resulting in fragmented communities and weakened democratic health.

As we reflect on these insights, it's evident that without concerted efforts to nurture social bonds and understanding, democracies risk further fragmentation. The challenges posed by economic disparities, cultural misunderstandings, and political tribalism all serve to exacerbate divisions, complicating governance and reducing resilience against external and internal pressures. A cohesive society, while seemingly elusive, remains vital for sustaining democratic principles. The road ahead demands pragmatic approaches that emphasize dialogue, inclusion, and shared purpose to overcome these barriers and restore faith in the democratic process.

# Reference List


Coleman, C. (2024, November 29). *The importance of social cohesion and communities*. House of Lords Library. https://lordslibrary.parliament.uk/the-importance-of-social-cohesion-and-communities/

Calvert, D. (2020, October 29). *The Political Divide in America Goes Beyond Polarization and Tribalism*. Kellogg School of Management. https://insight.kellogg.northwestern.edu/article/political-divide-america-beyond-polarization-tribalism-secularism

Diamond, L. (2004, February 10). *What Civil Society Can Do to Develop Democracy | Larry Diamond*. Diamond-Democracy.stanford.edu. https://diamond-democracy.stanford.edu/speaking/speeches/what-civil-society-can

-do-develop-democracy

Holtug, N. (2021, December 23). *Multiculturalism.* Academic.oup.com. https://doi.org/10.1093/oso/9780198797043.003.0009

*Multiculturalism and social cohesion.* (n.d.). OpenDemocracy. https://www.o pendemocracy.net/en/multiculturalism-and-social-cohesion/

*Resilience, Social Cohesion and Democracy: The Three Keys to Rebuilding Israel After 7 October.* (2024). Fathom. https://fathomjournal.org/resilience-soc ial-cohesion-and-democracy-the-three-keys-to-rebuilding-israel-after-7-october/

Runde, D. F., Bandura, R., & McLean, M. (2023, December 20). *Investing in Quality Education for Economic Development, Peace, and Stability.* Www.csis.org. https://www.csis.org/analysis/investing-quality-education-economic-development-peace-and-stability

*Reinforcing democracy initiative.* (2024). OECD. https://www.oecd.org/en/about/programmes/reinforcing-democracy-initiative.html

Tijerina, M. (2020, February 19). *Polarization, Partisanship, Tribalism, and Civility - Collin County Democrats.* Collin County Democrats. https://www.collindemocrats.org/civility/

Yudi Rusfiana, & Dewi Kurniasih. (2024, August 21). *The Role of Civil*

*Society Organizations in Promoting Social and Political Change in Indonesia.* Journal of Ethnic and Cultural Studies. https://doi.org/10.29333/ejecs/2154

# Income Inequality and Political Instability

Income inequality and political instability are closely intertwined, forming a complex relationship that affects societies worldwide. As economic disparities grow, they pose significant challenges to democratic systems, often shaking the foundations on which these societies rest. The widening gap between the wealthy and the less privileged fosters an environment of tension and division, further complicating efforts to maintain societal harmony. This chapter delves into how historical shifts and policy decisions have exacerbated these inequalities, influencing political landscapes in profound ways. From past decades characterized by economic booms and fairer wealth distribution to more recent times dominated by neoliberal policies, the transformation of economic dynamics has left an indelible mark on democratic stability.

In this exploration, we will examine the various stages of income inequality as they relate to political unrest, voter disenfranchisement, and policy effectiveness. Historical trends demonstrate the impact of economic policies on class structure and civic engagement, offering insight into how inequality can undermine social cohesion. Furthermore, we will investigate how economic disparities contribute to political alienation, spawning movements that challenge traditional power structures. By understanding the correlation between wealth concentration and civil dissatisfaction, we aim to shed light on the underlying factors driving political discord. This chapter also scrutinizes the role of taxation and wealth distribution in mitigating or exacerbating these issues, considering both the successes and failures of different approaches. Through this critical analysis, readers will gain a clearer picture of the persistent challenges faced by democracies grappling with economic inequality and its destabilizing effects.

## Historical Trends in Income Inequality

In examining the evolution of income inequality's influence on political stability, it is pivotal to consider how historical economic dynamics have shaped today's socio-political landscape. After World War II, many Western democracies experienced a period known as the Post-War Economic Boom, which significantly impacted civic engagement and social trust. During this era, economic policies favored the development of a robust middle class, enhancing societal cohesion and fostering stability within democratic institutions. This was evident in the increased participation in civic duties and institutions (Polacko, 2021). The prosperity of the middle class during this time created a sense of shared destiny among citizens, reducing friction between different social strata and promoting long-term democratic stability.

As with most things, however, the tide began to shift by the late 20th century. Neoliberalism emerged as a dominant economic philosophy, advocating for deregulation, reduced government intervention, and the privatization of public services. These policies were expected to foster economic growth by unleashing the potential of market forces. However, the reality was more complex. While some sectors indeed prospered, neoliberal practices also led to significant wealth disparities, creating a stark contrast between the wealthy elite and the remainder of the population. Deregulation enabled financial markets to benefit disproportionately from economic growth, while the privatization of essential services often left those unable to afford them disadvantaged, exacerbating existing inequalities. Consequently, the gap between the rich and poor widened considerably, undermining the earlier progress made in forming a cohesive, stable middle class (Gallo, 2017).

The onset of the 21st century brought further complications. The 2008 financial crisis marked a turning point, profoundly altering the economic and political environments of many countries. As economies struggled to recover, the measures taken frequently prioritized the top 1% of earners, further entrenching existing disparities. Government bailouts and financial incentives disproportionately benefited large corporations and wealthy individuals, leading to widespread public discontent. The recovery measures implemented after the crisis failed to address systemic issues or offer meaningful relief to those hardest hit by the recession, leaving large portions of the population feeling disenfranchised and mistrustful of governing institutions. As a result, the perceived disconnect between the political elite and ordinary citizens grew, fueling populist movements and increasing political polarization (Polacko, 2021).

Amid these challenges, it is essential to explore how other democracies have addressed income inequality through redistributive strategies, offering potential pathways for mitigating its adverse effects on political stability. For instance, several Nordic countries have implemented comprehensive welfare systems characterized by progressive taxation and robust social safety nets that aim to reduce income disparities. By ensuring access to quality education, healthcare, and social services, these nations have established environments where economic opportunity is more widely shared, contributing to greater political stability. Such models demonstrate that policy interventions can be effective in managing inequality and maintaining social cohesion, offering valuable insights for other democracies grappling with similar challenges (Gallo, 2017).

The examination of these various economic epochs and their impacts reflects a broader narrative about the relationship between income inequality and political stability. Historically, periods marked by economic equity and inclusivity have correlated with greater democratic strength and resilience. Conversely, policies that favor the concentration of wealth and limit economic mobility pose risks not only to economic health but also to democratic integrity. Understanding this evolution is crucial for developing policies aimed at fostering both economic equality and political stability.

The trajectory of income inequality and its political implications underscores the need for proactive and equitable policy measures. Rather than relying on short-term solutions or superficial remedies, there must be a concerted effort to address the structural factors contributing to economic disparities. This involves reassessing tax structures, enhancing labor protections, and investing in social services to create a more balanced economic environment. The experiences of countries that have successfully navigated these challenges highlight that achieving economic justice is not merely an altruistic goal but a foundational component of sustaining vibrant democracies.

## Correlation Between Economic Inequality and Political Unrest

Economic disparity has long been a precursor to political unrest, creating an intricate web of social and political challenges. Numerous studies demonstrate that when gaps between the wealthy and the poor widen, protests and strikes become more frequent. A telling example is provided by Massoud et al. (2019), who highlight that countries with higher economic inequality often experience intensified protest movements. These manifestations of public discontent frequently represent broader grievances about the imbalance in economic opportunities and access to resources.

The Arab Spring, a series of anti-government uprisings that swept through the Arab world starting in 2010, serves as a potent example of how socio-economic grievances can ignite systemic change. According to El-Haddad (2020), the breakdown of social contracts in several countries led to widespread disillusionment with corrupt systems that favored elites while neglecting the needs of the masses. In Tunisia and Egypt, this culminated in mass protests that demanded more equitable economic policies and structural reforms. The events underscored the powerful role economic disparity plays in fueling political upheaval when people perceive their futures are being compromised by entrenched elite interests.

The rise of populist movements across the globe can also be largely attributed to growing inequalities. Disenfranchised groups, feeling left behind by economic globalization and neoliberal policies, often turn to populist leaders who promise to disrupt the status quo. These leaders typically appeal to the anger and frustration felt by those who see few prospects for social mobility, fostering a narrative that pits "the people" against "the elite." This dynamic was evident in the United States and parts of Europe during significant political shifts in the past decade. Such movements thrive on highlighting the failures of existing democratic institutions to bridge economic divides and provide fair opportunities for all citizens.

Over time, persistent inequality does not just fuel temporary bouts of unrest but can lead to deeper political polarization that undermines the foundations of democracy itself. When large segments of the population feel alienated and voiceless, trust in democratic processes erodes. This often results in fragmented political landscapes where extreme ideologies find fertile ground, further destabilizing the political order. The dangers of entrenched inequality lie not only in immediate economic grievances but also in its ability to distort the political discourse, making constructive dialogue and consensus increasingly elusive.

To better understand the correlation between economic inequality and political unrest, it is important to view these issues within broader historical and geopolitical contexts. Patterns observed in various regions suggest that the relationship between income disparities and instability is complex and influenced by numerous factors, including governance quality, cultural norms, and the strength of civil society. Yet, the underlying theme remains consistent: societies with stark economic divides are more susceptible to upheavals that challenge their political frameworks.

Historically, periods of economic inequality have often been followed by demands for reform. During such times, marginalized groups seek redress through mechanisms like protests or political activism. While these movements sometimes result in positive changes that advance societal equity, they can also lead to unfavorable outcomes if exploited by opportunistic political actors. The potential for both progressive and regressive change highlights the dual-edged impact of inequality on political evolution.

In addition to inspiring political mobilization, rising inequality can also affect institutional integrity. Democratic institutions function optimally when there is broad-based confidence in fairness and inclusiveness. However, when wealth is concentrated in the hands of a few, it can skew policy priorities toward protecting privilege rather than promoting common welfare. This creates a vicious cycle where economic power translates into political influence, perpetuating inequality and exacerbating societal tensions.

To prevent the destabilizing effects of economic disparity, policymakers and civic leaders must address these challenges with comprehensive strategies that promote inclusive growth and equal opportunity. Efforts to reduce inequality must focus on strengthening social safety nets, ensuring access to quality education and healthcare, and fostering economic environments where entrepreneurship and innovation can thrive across all sectors of society. By addressing the root causes of inequality, societies can mitigate the risk of political unrest and cultivate a more resilient democratic framework.

## Impact on Voter Disenfranchisement

In contemporary democracies, the corrosive effects of income inequality on voter engagement are becoming increasingly pronounced. Economic barriers play a pivotal role in curtailing the ability of lower-income voters to participate in democratic processes. These barriers are multifaceted and manifest in various ways, including the costs associated with registration, accessing polling stations, and taking time off work to vote. For many low-income individuals, these costs can be prohibitive, effectively disenfranchising them. The financial burden placed on these individuals is a stark illustration of how economic resources, or the lack thereof, limit the civic empowerment of significant segments of the population.

Furthermore, the prevailing sense of economic hopelessness among low-income citizens exacerbates declines in voter participation. This demographic often perceives little to no improvement in their economic prospects, leading to disillusionment with political processes perceived as unresponsive to their needs. When people feel that their votes do not lead to meaningful change, they become less inclined to engage in voting. This cycle of disengagement perpetuates an entrenched system where only those with economic power can impact electoral outcomes, undermining the foundational principle of equal representation in a democracy.

The influence of economic elites on policy priorities further skews the democratic process, deepening the chasm of inequality. Those with substantial financial resources wield disproportionate influence over political agendas, often directing policy priorities to align with their interests. This dominance results in policies that exacerbate existing inequalities, neglecting basic social services and infrastructure improvements essential for lower-income groups. In turn, these neglected areas continue to depress voter turnout among economically disadvantaged communities, reinforcing a vicious cycle of disenfranchisement and inequality.

Grassroots initiatives, however, offer a beacon of hope by actively working to increase voter participation within marginalized communities. These initiatives operate on the ground level, building trust and engagement through direct outreach and education. They aim to remove barriers by helping individuals navigate the complexities of registration and voting, often providing transportation and childcare services to ease logistical challenges. By fostering a sense of agency and empowerment, grassroots movements help rekindle engagement among those historically sidelined by socioeconomic factors.

One notable effort comes from nonprofit organizations focusing on nonpartisan voter engagement, which have demonstrated success in boosting participation rates among underrepresented groups. According to data from Nonprofit VOTE's analysis, individuals engaged in these initiatives were markedly more likely to vote than their counterparts who were not involved (Supporting Nonpartisan Voter Engagement to Build a More Inclusive Democracy, 2024). Such engagement drives reflect a commitment to rebuilding democratic involvement from the ground up, ensuring that all voices, particularly those from disenfranchised communities, are heard in shaping the democratic future.

In terms of addressing the challenges posed by economic elites' influence, there is an urgent need for structural reforms that limit the ability of wealth to dictate political agendas. Implementing campaign finance reforms that restrict donations from powerful economic entities would help to level the playing field, allowing policy decisions to be shaped by broader public interest rather than narrow elite agendas. Furthermore, enhancing transparency about the sources of political funding could empower voters to make informed decisions, countering the skewed narratives often propagated by wealth-backed interests.

Philanthropic efforts also play a crucial role in bolstering the capacity of grassroots movements to effect change. By aligning funding with the core missions of community-based initiatives, philanthropists can empower these organizations to mount sustained voter engagement campaigns. As seen in strategies outlined by the Philanthropy for Voter Engagement toolkit, flexible funding models enable nonprofits to mobilize resources efficiently, focusing on long-term community empowerment rather than short electoral cycles (Supporting Nonpartisan Voter Engagement to Build a More Inclusive Democracy, 2024).

Yet, despite these efforts, significant challenges remain. Structural economic disparities continue to thwart full civic participation, necessitating comprehensive policy interventions aimed at reducing inequality and fostering genuine democratic engagement. Policymakers must prioritize creating equitable access to economic opportunities and dismantling systemic barriers hindering political participation. Without such deliberate actions, the promise of democracy remains unfulfilled for millions, locked out of a system designed to represent all.

## Economic Policy Failures and Successes

Growing economic disparities challenge democratic stability through their deep entanglement with national economic policies. Central to this dynamic is the effect of progressive taxation, which supports social programs designed to enhance democratic engagement. Progressive taxation ensures that wealthier citizens contribute a more significant share of their income towards funding government initiatives aimed at reducing inequality. By redistributing income in this way, societies strengthen their social fabric and mitigate the risks associated with extreme wealth concentration, such as disenfranchisement and political disengagement.

The importance of these tax structures cannot be understated. They provide essential revenue for public services like education, healthcare, and infrastructure—components that form the backbone of social stability. Economies relying on regressive tax systems, where lower-income families bear a disproportionate tax burden, often struggle to maintain these critical services adequately. As shown by Clements et al. (n.d.), when governments fail to implement fair tax policies, growing inequality can exacerbate tensions between different segments of the population, undermining the very foundations of democracy.

Moreover, well-designed welfare models play a crucial role in reducing poverty and promoting social stability. These systems are most effective when they offer comprehensive support tailored to address the needs of the disadvantaged. Welfare initiatives, such as unemployment benefits, housing assistance, and child care subsidies, aim to lift individuals out of poverty while providing a safety net during times of economic hardship. By investing in these programs, governments not only alleviate immediate financial pressures on vulnerable populations but also create long-term pathways for upward mobility and economic participation.

Countries that neglect robust welfare systems risk deepening socio-economic divides, leading to increased marginalization and potential civil unrest. Positive examples of welfare's impact are evident in nations with strong social safety nets, demonstrating lower rates of poverty and crime and higher levels of citizen satisfaction. This approach directly contributes to the health of democratic institutions by fostering social cohesion and ensuring that all citizens can participate fully in the democratic process.

Labor market regulations also play a pivotal role in determining income distribution within economies. Strong labor rights and protections ensure that workers receive fair wages and benefits commensurate with their efforts. Regulations such as minimum wage laws, workplace safety standards, and collective bargaining rights empower workers and reduce exploitative practices. When labor markets are balanced, with equitable opportunities for advancement and fair compensation, the resultant economic environment becomes more stable and inclusive.

Conversely, deregulation often leads to wage stagnation and job insecurity, primarily affecting low- and middle-income workers. This fosters an environment conducive to inequality, where capital accumulates among a privileged few, while the majority face escalating living costs without corresponding income increases. Regulatory frameworks that support equitable labor conditions are not only ethical imperatives but also strategic measures for maintaining societal balance and stability.

International trade agreements further influence domestic inequality, especially when they fail to prioritize workers' rights. While trade liberalization promises economic growth and resource efficiency, it can also widen the gap between rich and poor if improperly managed. Trade deals often prioritize corporate interests and profit margins over employee welfare, resulting in job displacement and downward pressure on wages. The Krist (2016) analysis reveals how unbalanced trade policies disproportionately favor capital owners, widening the chasm between them and the working class.

For international trade to positively impact inequality, agreements must include provisions protecting labor rights and enforcing fair trade practices. This involves establishing mechanisms to prevent exploitation and ensure that global economic integration benefits all, not just a select few. Policymakers must recognize the nuanced interplay between globalization and domestic economic realities, crafting agreements that facilitate mutual prosperity rather than perpetuating systemic inequities.

In assessing the impact of economic policies on inequality and democratic stability, it becomes apparent that failure to address these foundational issues carries significant risks. Economic policies wield the power to either ameliorate or exacerbate inequality, influencing the political landscape by shaping voter engagement, policy priorities, and trust in democratic institutions. Without intentional and thoughtful economic reforms, countries are likely to see an erosion of social capital and a rise in populism fueled by discontent and defeatism.

## Role of Taxation and Wealth Distribution

Taxation and wealth distribution are critical factors in addressing income inequality and ensuring political stability. Progressive taxation, where tax rates increase with income levels, plays a pivotal role in alleviating wealth concentration. By implementing a system where the wealthiest individuals contribute a larger share of their income, governments can mitigate the accumulation of excessive wealth in the hands of a few. This approach not only aids in reducing economic disparities but also fosters political stability by addressing grievances that arise from perceived unfairness in wealth distribution.

In practice, progressive taxation serves as a foundational pillar for redistributive policies aimed at promoting social equity. Countries that have adopted progressive tax models often exhibit lower levels of inequality. For instance, Nordic countries like Sweden and Denmark demonstrate the potential of such systems. With high tax rates for top earners, these nations have succeeded in narrowing income gaps and strengthening democratic institutions. Their tax revenues support robust public services and welfare programs, creating a society where citizens feel more secure and valued. This sense of collective welfare contributes to political cohesion and reduces the likelihood of unrest caused by social divides.

Beyond progressive taxation, wealth taxes and basic income programs emerge as innovative tools to empower economically marginalized groups. Wealth taxes, which impose levies on assets rather than just income, help target accumulated wealth that remains untaxed under traditional income tax systems. By taxing property, investments, and other assets, governments can generate additional revenue for redistributive efforts. This measure ensures that those with substantial holdings contribute fairly to societal welfare, addressing both immediate income disparities and long-term wealth accumulation.

Basic income programs, where all citizens receive a regular, unconditional financial grant, represent another promising approach. These initiatives aim to provide a safety net for all individuals, ensuring a basic standard of living.

By offering financial security to those most vulnerable, basic income schemes can alleviate poverty and reduce reliance on traditional welfare systems. Such programs have gained attention globally, with pilot projects underway in various regions. The outcomes suggest that basic income not only supports economic stability but also empowers recipients, granting them the freedom to pursue education or entrepreneurship without the constant pressure of financial insecurity.

The ethical dimensions of taxation are often rooted in social contract theories, which highlight the importance of fair contributions to society. According to these theories, citizens consent to taxation as part of their agreement with the state, expecting reciprocal benefits in the form of public goods and services. Fair taxation is viewed as a moral obligation, ensuring that everyone pays their due share while benefiting from societal progress. This ethical perspective reinforces the need for transparency and accountability in tax systems, instilling trust in government actions.

The success of redistributive policies can be further understood through a comparative analysis of international practices. The Nordic model stands out as a benchmark for effective redistribution, characterized by extensive cash transfers and comprehensive welfare programs. These countries prioritize equity and inclusivity, leveraging high taxation to fund services that benefit all citizens. Education, healthcare, and childcare are universally accessible, reducing inequality and enhancing social mobility. Consequently, Nordic societies boast high levels of social trust and civic engagement, demonstrating how equitable policies contribute to democratic resilience.

However, the implementation of taxation and wealth distribution mechanisms faces significant challenges. Economic globalization, technological advancements, and changing labor markets present obstacles to maintaining fair tax systems. Multinational corporations often exploit loopholes to evade taxes, exacerbating income disparities. Therefore, international cooperation is crucial in enforcing tax compliance and closing gaps that allow wealth to escape regulatory oversight. Harmonizing tax policies across borders can prevent a race to the bottom, where countries compete to offer lower tax rates, ultimately undermining global efforts to address inequality.

Despite the theoretical benefits of progressive taxation and redistributive policies, practical implementation requires careful consideration. Policymakers must balance revenue generation with economic competitiveness, avoiding measures that discourage investment or stifle growth. Crafting effective tax policies involves navigating complex political landscapes, where vested interests may resist changes that threaten their financial advantages. Transparent dialogue between governments and citizens is essential to building consensus and ensuring that taxation serves the broader goal of societal well-being.

## Insights and Implications

This chapter delves into the persistent and troubling connection between economic disparities and the fragility of democratic systems. By tracing the historical and current trends, it becomes evident that income inequality remains a potent disruptor of political stability. From post-war prosperity to the neoliberal shifts of the late 20th century, widening income gaps have left a lasting impact on the civic landscape. The financial downturns of the 21st century only deepened these divides, fueling populist movements and eroding trust in institutions meant to safeguard democratic ideals. These insights raise significant concerns about the sustainability of democracies when faced with unchecked economic inequality.

Addressing these issues requires comprehensive policy changes aimed at reducing income disparities and restoring democratic engagement. Redistributive strategies, such as progressive taxation and robust social safety nets, are crucial yet often challenging to implement amidst globalized economies and resistant political forces. Without firm action, the very structure of democracy risks faltering under the weight of unequal economic power. Understanding the interplay between wealth concentration and political unrest is vital for politically engaged readers and scholars trying to navigate and remedy these complex dynamics. As history has shown, neglect of these inequalities only heightens instability and undermines democratic integrity.

# Reference List

Clements, B., Mooij, R. de, Francese, M., Gupta, S., & Keen, M. (n.d.). *Chapter 1. Fiscal Policy and Income Inequality: An Overview*. Www.elibrary.imf.org; International Monetary Fund. https://www.elibrary.imf.org/view/book/9781513531625/ch001.xml

Clavería, O., & Petar Sorić. (2023, November 2). *Inequality and redistribution: evidence from Scandinavian and Mediterranean countries*. Applied Economic Analysis; Emerald Publishing Limited. https://doi.org/10.1108/aea-06-2023-0201

El-Haddad, A. (2020, March 1). *Redefining the social contract in the wake of the Arab Spring: The experiences of Egypt, Morocco and Tunisia*. World Development. https://doi.org/10.1016/j.worlddev.2019.104774

Gallo, A. (2017, November 9). *How the American dream turned into greed and inequality*. World Economic Forum. https://www.weforum.org/stories/2017/11/the-pursuit-of-happiness-how-the-american-dream-turned-into-greed-and-inequality/

Krist, W. (2016). *Trade Agreements and Economic Theory*. Wilson Center. https://www.wilsoncenter.org/chapter-3-trade-agreements-and-economic-theory

Maye, A. (2023, August 1). *Chasing the dream of equity: How policy has shaped racial economic disparities*. Economic Policy Institute. https://www.epi.org/

publication/chasing-the-dream-of-equity/

Massoud, T. G., Doces, J. A., & Magee, C. (2019, July). *Protests and the Arab Spring: An Empirical Investigation.* Polity. https://doi.org/10.1086/704001

Polacko, M. (2021, October 20). *Causes and Consequences of Income Inequality – An Overview.* Statistics, Politics and Policy. https://doi.org/10.1515/spp-2021-0017

Ringen, S., & Uusitalo, H. (1990). *Income Distribution and Redistribution in the Nordic Welfare States.* International Journal of Sociology; Taylor & Francis, Ltd.; JSTOR. https://doi.org/10.2307/20630040

*Supporting nonpartisan voter engagement to build a more inclusive democracy.* (2024, July 23). Candid Insights. https://blog.candid.org/post/nonpartisan-voter-engagement-for-a-more-inclusive-democracy/

# Economic Crises and Their Aftermath

Economic crises are pivotal events that reshape societies and expose vulnerabilities in democratic systems. When economies falter, the ripple effects extend far beyond immediate financial distress, reaching into the very fabric of political and social structures. The aftermath of such downturns often sees a weakening of trust in democratic norms, as people grapple with both tangible hardships and the perception of systemic failures. These disruptions are not just temporary; they can set off a chain reaction that challenges the core principles of democracy. During these times, citizens question the effectiveness of their governments, and long-standing beliefs in democratic ideals are tested by economic realities.

As this chapter unfolds, it delves into the complex ways economic crises affect democratic institutions and the erosion of public confidence in governance. It explores how governmental responses—or lack thereof—during financial turmoil can exacerbate socio-political divides and cultivate environments ripe for populism and authoritarianism. By examining historical and contemporary examples, the chapter highlights the interconnectedness of economic policy, cultural unrest, and political disillusionment. Readers will gain insight into how economic adversity sharpens societal tensions and contributes to shifts in political landscapes, often inviting voters to reconsider traditional allegiances and the very concept of representation in a democracy. Through this exploration, the chapter aims to provide a clearer understanding of why safeguarding democratic integrity during economic downturns is crucial yet challenging.

## The Catalyzing Effect of the 2008 Financial Crisis on Democratic Institutions

The 2008 financial crisis marked a turning point for democratic institutions worldwide, catalyzing significant political and social shifts. One of the most profound impacts was the erosion of public trust in governmental and financial institutions. As banks faltered and economies crumbled, citizens' confidence in the democratic processes underpinning these systems weakened. This decline stemmed from the perception that governmental interventions favored financial elites at the expense of ordinary citizens. Many people believed that bailouts and financial rescue plans primarily benefited wealthy individuals and corporations, leaving everyday citizens to bear the brunt of austerity measures and economic contraction.

The widening chasm between promises made by elected officials and the stark realities perceived by the populace exacerbated feelings of systemic injustice. Government responses were often seen as inadequate or even complicit in maintaining economic inequality. As austerity measures took hold, the burden of economic recovery disproportionately affected lower-income populations, deepening divides and seeding discontent. For many, the crisis underscored a fundamental inequity entrenched within their societies—one that perpetually privileges the affluent while marginalizing those already struggling. This pervasive sense of injustice fueled anger and resentment, further destabilizing faith in democratic governance.

As traditional forms of political representation seemed incapable of addressing these grievances, there was a notable disruption in party alignments across various democracies. Disillusionment with mainstream political establishments paved the way for the rise of populist movements, which capitalized on anti-establishment sentiments. These new political forces tapped into widespread frustrations, positioning themselves as champions of the 'common people' against perceived corrupt elites. Populism, in its various forms, offered an appealing alternative to many who felt abandoned by conventional politics. This shift challenged existing party structures, introducing new dynamics to electoral competition and complicating the landscape of democratic representation.

Economic hardship not only reshaped political affiliations but also exacerbated cultural conflicts. The intertwining of economic narratives with cultural grievances became increasingly evident during and after the crisis. Economic distress amplified issues such as immigration, national sovereignty, and identity politics, creating fertile ground for polarizing debates. Cultural divisions, once simmering beneath the surface, began to emerge more prominently. These tensions further fragmented societies, often leading to heightened polarization and distrust among differing cultural groups.

In Europe, the Eurozone crisis highlighted these fractures dramatically. Countries hit hardest by economic turmoil faced increased skepticism towards transnational projects such as the European Union. In some regions, citizens questioned whether alignment with broader European agendas truly served their interests or simply benefited stronger economies at the cost of their own national wellbeing (Passari, 2020). This skepticism offered opportunities for anti-European sentiments to flourish, bolstering parties advocating for nationalism and xenophobia.

Across the Atlantic, similar patterns emerged. In the United States, the financial crisis coincided with long-standing economic anxieties, further eroding trust in political institutions. Many Americans saw the government's inability—or unwillingness—to prevent or adequately respond to the crisis as evidence of a fractured and ineffective system (Diamond, 2017). These attitudes galvanized support for candidates who promised dramatic departures from established political norms, including nativist and illiberal populisms.

Furthermore, the crisis's repercussions extended beyond immediate economic implications to influence social media landscapes. As digital platforms gained traction, they became vehicles for magnifying dissatisfaction and mobilizing disaffected citizens. Social media facilitated the rapid spread of populist rhetoric, amplifying narratives of corruption and disenfranchisement. This digital evolution played a crucial role in shaping contemporary political discourse, often bypassing traditional media gatekeepers and promoting divisive messages directly to vast audiences.

While the 2008 financial crisis undeniably accelerated these trends, it also underscored vulnerabilities within democracies that predated the economic meltdown. Trust in political institutions and confidence in democratic processes had already been declining in many parts of the world, driven by various factors including globalization, technological change, and cultural shifts. However, the crisis acted as a catalyst, bringing these underlying issues into sharper focus and prompting urgent questions about the future of democracy.

The lessons from this period underscore the ongoing challenge that economic crises pose to democratic resilience. They highlight the need for robust mechanisms capable of mitigating inequalities and rebuilding trust amidst adversity. Addressing the root causes of economic disparity and ensuring fair distribution of resources and opportunities remain critical tasks for sustaining democratic institutions in times of crisis. Moreover, fostering inclusive dialogue across disparate cultural and political lines is essential for bridging divides and restoring faith in democratic governance.

## Link Between Economic Downturns and Cultural Unrest

Economic downturns have historically been catalysts for cultural unrest and a challenge to democratic norms. When economies contract, societies often experience a surge of social movements and civil tension. Historical evidence underlines that economic recessions frequently coincide with protests and widespread dissent. For example, the Great Depression of the 1930s saw the rise of various social movements as populations struggled with unemployment and poverty, putting pressure on democratic institutions to respond effectively.

Income disparities during these periods often exacerbate feelings of alienation among different groups within a society. In times of economic stress, the gaps between the haves and have-nots become more pronounced, leading to increased resentment and division. This alienation can manifest in support for identity politics and extremism, as people seek to assert their identity and protect their interests. For instance, during economic crises, marginalized communities may rally around identity-centric movements as a response to perceived grievances and inequalities. Such conditions offer fertile ground for extremist ideologies to take root, promising radical solutions and simple answers to complex economic problems.

Furthermore, economic crises often lead to an attraction toward authoritarian solutions. As citizens grapple with instability and insecurity, they may turn to leaders or political systems that promise quick fixes and decisive action. History provides numerous examples of how economic hardship paves the way for authoritarian regimes to gain power by presenting themselves as capable of restoring order and stability. The appeal of authoritarianism lies in its apparent efficiency and the promise of rapid economic recovery, even at the expense of democratic principles and freedoms.

Additionally, economic stress contributes to heightened cultural polarization within societies. During downturns, existing cultural divisions are amplified as economic struggles force individuals and groups to compete for limited resources. This competition further entrenches divisions, reinforcing stereotypes and prejudices rather than fostering unity. Cultural polarization is particularly dangerous because it erodes the social fabric necessary for a functioning democracy. Instead of collaboration and compromise, polarized societies tend to be characterized by confrontation and conflict.

The interplay between economic crises and the erosion of democratic norms highlights a critical vulnerability in modern democracies. As noted by some experts, affective polarization has been a concern as it leads to communities viewing each other as threatening and immoral (Kleinfeld, 2023). This perception deepens during economic turmoil, where the stakes feel higher and cooperation seems less attainable. Economist studies suggest that when political and opinion leaders exploit this polarization for strategic gains, it can exacerbate societal rifts and contribute to a climate of hostility and intolerance.

Moreover, income inequality exacerbated by economic downturns plays a pivotal role in stirring cultural unrest. Disparities fuel discontent and drive societal factions apart, undermining trust in democratic processes. As the gap widens during recessions, those who feel left behind or marginalized by economic policies are more likely to distrust democratic institutions that seem to fail in delivering equitable outcomes (Challenges to Democracy | Inequality, Identity Politics, Authoritarianism, & Facts | Britannica, 2023). When people believe the system is rigged against them, they may withdraw from democratic participation, leading to weakening civic engagement and increasing susceptibility to anti-democratic ideas.

In this context, historical patterns reveal that responses to economic crises vary significantly between nations. Successful navigations often involve comprehensive policy approaches that address both immediate economic needs and underlying social tensions. Such interventions need to encompass not just economic relief but also initiatives aimed at bridging cultural divides and promoting inclusivity. However, when governments fail to act decisively, public disillusionment grows, potentially pushing citizens towards authoritarian alternatives that appear more decisive.

## Impact of Government Responses on Democratic Health

In times of economic crises, governments hold significant sway over the resilience and integrity of democratic systems. The actions taken by these administrations either mitigate the damage or exacerbate the erosion of trust in democratic ideals. Effective policy interventions are paramount. When governments respond with measures that visibly alleviate economic distress, they can restore public confidence and strengthen democratic institutions. For instance, during the 2008 financial downturn, countries like Germany implemented robust fiscal stimulus packages that helped to buffer their economies against severe recessionary impacts. Such actions not only addressed immediate economic woes but also reinforced the public's belief in their government's capability to manage crises effectively (Jurado & Navarrete, 2021).

On the flip side, ineffective or poorly executed policies can lead to disillusionment. If the public perceives that government responses favor select groups or fail to adequately address the needs of the broader population, trust in democratic institutions diminishes. This deterioration is particularly pronounced when there is a noticeable disparity between policy rhetoric and tangible outcomes. For example, austerity measures in certain European countries during the same period were seen as disproportionately affecting lower-income citizens, leading to widespread protests and greater skepticism about governmental intentions and fairness (The Policy Circle, 2016). Such perceptions of unfairness contribute significantly to civic disengagement, weakening the very foundations of democracy.

Public perception plays a crucial role in this dynamic. When people believe that government actions are equitable and just, they are more likely to engage civically and support democratic processes. Conversely, if disparities remain unaddressed and citizens feel marginalized, skepticism grows. This skepticism was evident in Greece during its debt crisis; citizens' faith in their government's ability to address inequalities was eroded, contributing to decreased civic engagement and an uptick in support for radical political alternatives. The feeling of being unheard or neglected fosters disenchantment with the status quo, prompting some individuals to seek solutions outside traditional democratic frameworks (Turnbull-Dugarte and Stuart, 2020).

Inaction during economic crises poses perhaps the greatest threat to democratic health. When governments fail to act decisively, they risk political upheaval. Citizens, frustrated by perceived governmental impotence, often turn to extreme ideologies or populist leaders who promise swift resolutions. This is partly because inaction reinforces feelings of helplessness and loss of control, both of which are antithetical to democratic engagement. The rise of populism in several European nations post-2008 can be attributed, in part, to perceived governmental inaction and inadequate crisis management, which left many citizens feeling alienated and disenfranchised (Magalhães, 2014; Cordero and Simón, 2016).

A comparative analysis further underscores the importance of proactive governance. Countries that successfully navigate economic crises often emerge with strengthened democratic institutions. These nations typically adopt comprehensive and inclusive strategies that address both economic recovery and social cohesion. For instance, Iceland's response to the financial collapse involved holding those responsible accountable while simultaneously implementing innovative social policies. This approach not only staved off potential for deep political rifts but also rebuilt public trust in national institutions. By contrast, countries that struggled or delayed in their responses faced prolonged periods of political instability and weakened democratic norms (Devine, 2021).

The evidence from these varied experiences suggests several guidelines for enhancing democratic resilience during economic crises. Firstly, transparent communication and inclusive policymaking processes are essential. When citizens understand the rationale behind government actions and see diverse perspectives considered, they are more likely to perceive the process as fair and legitimate. Governments should prioritize policies that equitably distribute resources and opportunities, ensuring that no significant segments of the population consistently bear the brunt of economic hardship. Additionally, fostering civic dialogue and participation can help maintain engagement, even in challenging times. By involving citizens in decision-making processes, trust and collaboration between the state and its people can be cultivated, thus safeguarding democratic principles at a foundational level.

## Long-term Impacts of Economic Crises on Political Trust

The enduring effects of economic crises on political trust within democracies represent a significant challenge, as reflected in numerous studies. Economic downturns often lead to declines in public trust that outlast the financial recovery period. Trust indicators lag behind because people remember the hardships endured during crises, which impacts their confidence in democratic institutions (DER & ERKEL, 2023). The aftermath of the Great Recession, for instance, illustrated how prolonged economic instability can shadow governmental efforts to restore faith even as economies improve. This phenomenon is not merely about temporary disillusionment but reflects deeper, long-lasting scars on the social fabric.

In times of economic turmoil, the instinct for self-preservation often takes precedence over civic engagement, creating a barrier to active political participation. When individuals are preoccupied with meeting basic needs, the motivation and resources to engage civically diminish. As citizens prioritize immediate survival concerns, they may become less involved in political processes, leading to reduced turnout in elections and lower participation in community initiatives (When Trust Becomes a Luxury: How Economic Crises Undermine Political Trust among the Most Disadvantaged, n.d.). This withdrawal from civic life presents a risk of weakening democratic structures, as it narrows the channels through which governments receive feedback and accountability from their constituents.

Furthermore, economic crises can significantly impact generational trust. Younger populations, who witness economic volatility at formative stages in their lives, often develop a lasting skepticism towards democracy. A prevalent sentiment of distrust can grow among youth, who view democracy as incapable of providing stability or opportunities. This skepticism tends to persist into adulthood, shaping a generation less inclined to believe in or engage with democratic processes. The experience of seeing their prospects diminished by economic downturns can lead to a belief that democratic systems are inherently flawed, fostering disengagement and raising questions about future commitments to uphold democratic values (Marien, 2011; Van Erkel & Van der Meer, 2016).

Economic crises have historically reshaped political dynamics, presenting substantial risks to the maintenance of democratic norms. Governments struggling to steer their nations through turbulent times may face pressures that encourage shortcuts in governance, undermining transparency and accountability. Such environments can be ripe for populist movements, which exploit public dissatisfaction and propose authoritarian solutions as quick fixes. These movements capitalize on the erosion of trust, promoting narratives that democratic processes are inefficient or corrupt. As seen in parts of Europe after the Great Recession, the rise of euroscepticism is an example of how economic hardship can catalyze shifts towards anti-establishment sentiments (Ellinas & Lamprianou, 2014; Torcal, 2014).

The legacy of fractured trust can endure, influencing the trajectory of political systems long after a crisis has ended. As policymakers grapple with current challenges, they must recognize the importance of rebuilding trust as a cornerstone of democratic resilience. Efforts to restore confidence require more than just economic recovery; they necessitate transparent governance, inclusive policy-making, and active engagement with all societal segments, especially those most affected by economic downdrafts. Without addressing these deeper issues, the foundations of democracy remain vulnerable to future crises, potentially leading to further erosion of trust and participation (DER & ERKEL, 2023).

Regaining trust also involves acknowledging and mitigating the disproportionate impacts felt by disadvantaged groups during economic crises. These groups tend to suffer more, lacking resources to buffer against financial shocks, which exacerbates their sense of alienation from political systems perceived as inattentive to their needs. Policymakers must focus on equity-oriented strategies that cushion the blow of downturns and provide targeted support to those most in need. By doing so, they can begin to mend the fractures in trust and improve civic engagement across diverse populations (When Trust Becomes a Luxury: How Economic Crises Undermine Political Trust among the Most Disadvantaged, n.d.).

## Lessons and Safeguards for Strengthening Democracy

In exploring the lessons from past economic crises and their implications for democracy, one must first consider the importance of proactive governance. The propensity for societal unrest during economic downturns highlights the need for preparedness measures to mitigate potential slides toward authoritarianism. Quoting former President Barack Obama, "Our democracy is not a given. It requires our active participation, vigilance, and above all, our commitment to the common good" (Staff, 2024). This serves as a reminder that maintaining democratic norms is a continuous effort. Economic tumult can create openings for authoritarian inclinations when governments appear unresponsive or ineffective. Therefore, establishing frameworks that anticipate and address these challenges head-on is crucial.

A key aspect of these preventive strategies involves policy innovations. By enhancing transparency in government operations and fostering cross-party collaboration, democracies can become more resilient against destabilizing forces. According to Senator Elizabeth Warren, "In times of uncertainty, preparation and vigilance are our strongest defenses" (Staff, 2024). In aligning with this sentiment, democracies should prioritize policies that encourage open communication and accountability. This not only builds trust among citizens but also helps ensure that decisions reflecting public interests are made even amidst crisis scenarios.

Moreover, community engagement initiatives serve as critical pillars in strengthening democratic structures. Empowering citizens through local solutions not only increases trust in governmental institutions but also fortifies society against divisive ideologies that tend to emerge during periods of economic strain. As highlighted by Senator Cory Booker, "Our democracy depends on each and every one of us standing up and being counted" (Staff, 2024). Encouraging civic engagement at grassroots levels provides avenues for people to actively participate in shaping the political landscape, thereby reinforcing the democratic process.

The necessity of future-proofing democracy demands embedding safeguards such as independent assessments and robust civic education programs. As highlighted in the discussions about private sector commitments to advancing democracy, proactive steps are essential to protect democratic principles (Private Sector Commitments to Advance Democracy, n.d.). Incorporating independent evaluations into the fabric of governance ensures that checks and balances remain effective. Furthermore, enhancing civic education prepares citizens to critically engage with political developments, fostering an informed electorate that can discern manipulative tactics aimed at undermining democratic integrity.

However, efforts to future-proof democracy must extend beyond mere institutional changes. They require a cultural shift towards embracing the complexities inherent in governance while remaining committed to unity and progress. This perspective resonates with Dr. Jill Biden's assertion that "Voting is not just our right; it is our responsibility" (Staff, 2024). Civic education fosters this understanding, equipping individuals with the tools needed to navigate the intricacies of democratic systems and recognize the significance of their participation.

## Bringing It All Together

The chapter has explored the unsettling relationship between economic crises and the erosion of democratic norms, emphasizing how financial turmoil undermines public trust and fosters disillusionment. As citizens perceive that governments prioritize financial elites over everyday people, this perceived favoritism breeds skepticism towards established institutions. The widening income gap exacerbates feelings of inequality, fueling populist movements and cultural divisions that threaten democratic stability. Economic downturns also worsen cultural polarization as communities compete for limited resources, deepening societal divides and paving the way for authoritarian tendencies. These dynamics underscore the grim reality that democracies face significant challenges in maintaining resilience amid economic instability.

In light of these findings, it becomes clear that the road to preserving democracy is fraught with challenges. Governments must mitigate economic inequalities and restore trust among citizens through transparent and equitable policies. However, the pessimistic view remains that without significant reforms, economic crises will continue to destabilize societies and undermine democratic values. The persistent distrust and disconnection felt by many citizens serve as reminders of democracy's fragility in times of economic stress. It is essential, yet daunting, to address these tensions proactively to prevent further deterioration of democratic norms. Ultimately, the onus lies on both political leaders and engaged citizens to navigate these turbulent waters, ensuring democracy's survival even when faced with seemingly insurmountable obstacles.

# Reference List


*Challenges to democracy | Inequality, Identity Politics, Authoritarianism, & Facts | Britannica.* (2023, July 12). Www.britannica.com. https://www.britannica.com/topic/challenges-to-democracy

DER, V., & ERKEL, P. F. A. V. (2023, December 20). *Moving beyond the political trust crisis debate: Residual analyses to understand trends in political trust.* European Journal of Political Research; Wiley. https://doi.org/10.1111/1475-6765.12645

Diamond, L. (2017). *When Does Populism Become a Threat to Democracy? | Larry Diamond.* Diamond-Democracy.stanford.edu; Stanford University. https://diamond-democracy.stanford.edu/speaking/speeches/when-does-populism-become-threat-democracy

Jurado, I., & Navarrete, R. M. (2021, August 11). *Economic Crisis and Attitudes Towards Democracy: How Ideology Moderates Reactions to Economic Downturns.* Frontiers in Political Science. https://doi.org/10.3389/fpos.2021.685199

Kleinfeld, R. (2023). *Polarization, Democracy, and Political Violence in the United States: What the Research Says.* Carnegie Endowment for International Peace. https://carnegieendowment.org/research/2023/09/polarization-democracy-and-political-violence-in-the-united-states-what-the-research-says

*Private Sector Commitments to Advance Democracy.* (n.d.). United States

Department of State. https://www.state.gov/private-sector-commitments-to-advance-democracy/

Passari, E. (2020). *The Great Recession and the Rise of Populism*. Intereconomics. https://www.intereconomics.eu/contents/year/2020/number/1/article/the-great-recession-and-the-rise-of-populism.html

Staff, J. (2024, August 21). *Unity, Resilience, and Democracy: Lessons from the 2024 DNC for Emergency Management and Beyond*. Juvare. https://www.juvare.com/unity-resilience-and-democracy-lessons-from-the-2024-dnc-for-emergency-management-and-beyond/

The Policy Circle. (2016). *Civic Engagement - The Policy Circle*. The Policy Circle. https://www.thepolicycircle.org/brief/whats-whys-civic-engagement/

*When trust becomes a luxury: How economic crises undermine political trust among the most disadvantaged*. (n.d.). Jacques Delors Centre. https://www.delorscentre.eu/en/publications/political-trust-in-economic-crisis

# Potential for Renewal

The potential for renewal in liberal democracies is complex and fraught with obstacles. It's not enough to rely on the old frameworks of governance; contemporary challenges require fresh strategies that extend beyond traditional paradigms. In recent years, many have expressed concern over increasing polarization and stagnation within democratic institutions. The entrenched power structures resist change, often prioritizing their interests over the collective good. These dynamics create an environment where true revitalization seems elusive, leaving citizens disillusioned with the political process. As governments struggle to adapt to social and technological advances, maintaining public trust becomes even more challenging. Therefore, the quest for democratic renewal must contend with these formidable barriers to pave the way for a more equitable society.

This chapter delves into the various avenues for reinvigorating liberal democracy amidst such pessimistic realities. It examines historical precedents, highlighting how past crises have sometimes spurred innovation and adaptation in democratic practices. By scrutinizing examples from history, we can uncover lessons applicable to today's context. Additionally, this exploration includes an analysis of contemporary efforts aiming to address systemic inequities through new governance models. The focus lies on fostering inclusive participation, dismantling existing barriers to engagement, and empowering marginalized voices. Through an expository lens, this chapter seeks to unravel the intricate web of factors influencing democratic renewal, providing insights that are both critical and reflective.

## Concept of a 'Third Founding'

The potential for a new foundational moment in democracy is both a daunting challenge and an optimistic opportunity, hinging on the necessity to reimagine democratic principles that can guide us through contemporary struggles. Historically, American democracy has evolved during times of crisis, where pivotal transformations have redefined its core values and functioning. From the post-Civil War reconstruction to the Civil Rights Movement, these periods were characterized by an urgency to address systemic inequities and reinvigorate public engagement with democratic ideals (Kleinfeld, 2022).

The notion of a 'third founding' suggests a necessary evolution that prioritizes equity and inclusion as central tenets of modern democracy. In our current climate, this could mean developing governance structures that engage citizens in meaningful ways, allowing them to actively contribute to the reshaping of democratic practices. This reimagined democracy would be more participatory, ensuring that diverse voices are not just heard but also influential in policy-making processes. Such transformation demands an intentional shift towards inclusivity, challenging traditional power structures and amplifying marginalized voices to create a more equitable society.

However, achieving this transformation is fraught with significant challenges. Resistance from entrenched interests, who benefit from maintaining the status quo, poses a formidable barrier. This resistance often manifests in political polarization, where divisive rhetoric and actions serve to entrench existing divides rather than bridge them. The current political landscape, marked by stark ideological divisions, makes it difficult to achieve consensus on fundamental changes necessary for democratic revitalization (Democracy in Crisis, 2019). These divisions not only hinder legislative progress but also erode public trust in democratic institutions, creating an environment where democratic deterioration can thrive unchecked.

Yet, amid these challenges lies the potential for hope and renewal. Imagining a revitalized democracy requires fostering a sense of hope and participation across various demographics. Empowering citizens to envision and work towards a shared future can spark a collective movement towards democratic renewal. Encouraging active civic participation across age, race, and socio-economic backgrounds ensures that democracy remains vibrant and responsive to the needs of all its constituents.

In doing so, there must be concerted efforts to dismantle systemic barriers that hinder participation, such as voter suppression tactics and gerrymandering, which disproportionately affect minority communities. Addressing these issues not only enhances equity but also strengthens the overall democratic fabric by ensuring that every voice counts equally.

A guideline for addressing these challenges includes developing comprehensive strategies that engage citizens directly in the democratic process. This involves creating platforms for dialogue and collaboration that transcend partisan lines, allowing for the exchange of ideas and fostering mutual understanding. Initiatives that promote civic education and empowerment can also play a crucial role in building a resilient democratic society. Educating individuals about their rights and responsibilities as citizens encourages informed participation and cultivates a culture of accountability and transparency.

Moreover, leveraging technology can be instrumental in enhancing democratic participation. Digital platforms offer unprecedented opportunities to connect and mobilize citizens, facilitating greater involvement in political discourse and decision-making processes. By using technology to bridge gaps and foster connections, we can create a more inclusive and dynamic democratic system that is responsive to the needs of its people (Kleinfeld, 2022).

Central to this renewed democratic vision is the promotion of equity and inclusion as guiding principles. Policies that address systemic inequalities and promote social justice are essential in creating a fair and just society. This includes implementing measures that ensure equal access to education, healthcare, and economic opportunities, laying the groundwork for a society where everyone can thrive.

Furthermore, fostering a culture of empathy and understanding is vital in bridging divides and overcoming polarization. Encouraging dialogue and collaboration among diverse groups can help break down stereotypes and misconceptions, fostering a sense of community and shared purpose. By building bridges across differences, we can create a cohesive society that values diversity and embraces pluralism as strengths, rather than liabilities.

## Examples of Democratic Renewal from History

Throughout history, democratic renewal has emerged from moments of crisis and transformation, offering lessons and inspiration for contemporary society. One profound example is the reconstruction era that followed World War II, which laid the groundwork for peace and cooperation in Europe. This period saw the establishment of robust social safety nets within many countries, as they recognized the vital importance of protecting their citizens against future upheavals. Nations like Germany and France, once fierce adversaries, began to forge alliances, leading to regional cooperation mechanisms such as the European Coal and Steel Community. This economic interdependence not only advanced prosperity but also fostered enduring political stability, setting a precedent for modern European integration.

The American civil rights movement provides another testament to the power of grassroots activism in catalyzing systemic change. Sparked by determined individuals and communities, this movement challenged deep-seated racial injustices and demanded equality. Leaders like Martin Luther King Jr., Rosa Parks, and many other unsung heroes rallied people across the nation to push for significant legal reforms. Their efforts culminated in landmark legislation, including the Civil Rights Act of 1964 and the Voting Rights Act of 1965, transforming American society by dismantling segregation and securing voting rights for African Americans. The movement stresses the potential impact of collective action in demanding democratic reforms and overcoming entrenched inequalities.

South Africa's transition from apartheid to democracy stands as a powerful illustration of reconciliation and international collaboration. For decades, the apartheid regime enforced racial segregation, met with widespread internal resistance and global criticism. The dismantling of this oppressive system involved complex negotiations and the granting of equal rights to all citizens. Under Nelson Mandela's leadership, the Truth and Reconciliation Commission (TRC) played a pivotal role in healing the nation's wounds by confronting past atrocities and promoting national unity. This process demonstrated the importance of dialogue, forgiveness, and international support in achieving democratic renewal. The global community's solidarity, exemplified by sanctions and diplomacy, was crucial in this transition, underscoring how international pressure can aid domestic struggles for justice (Britannica, 2019).

The fall of the Iron Curtain in Eastern Europe offers further insights into citizen mobilization catalyzing political reform. As Communist regimes crumbled under the weight of popular discontent, waves of protests swept through the region. In Poland, the Solidarity movement, led by Lech Wałęsa, galvanized workers and intellectuals alike, forcing the government to negotiate and eventually allow free elections. Similarly, Czechoslovakia experienced the Velvet Revolution, where peaceful demonstrations ended four decades of authoritarian rule. These events highlighted the resilience and determination of citizens who yearned for freedom and democracy, proving that unified, nonviolent action can topple even the most entrenched regimes. The rise of democratic governments across Eastern Europe showcased the global appeal of democratic values, prompting a reassessment of political systems worldwide.

The exploration of these examples underscores a common theme: the renewal of democracy hinges on the proactive engagement of citizens, institutions, and international allies. Each instance reveals unique strategies and adaptations to local contexts, yet all share a commitment to justice, liberty, and equitable governance. They remind us that while the path to democratic renewal may be fraught with challenges, it is achievable through perseverance and collective will. These historical precedents serve as beacons of hope, providing blueprints for societies aiming to revitalize democratic ideals in today's complex political landscape (Galston, 2018).

Reflecting on these lessons is increasingly pertinent as contemporary democracies face both internal and external challenges. Internally, populist movements seek to divide, exploiting socioeconomic grievances and fostering distrust in traditional institutions. Externally, autocratic regimes threaten to undermine democratic norms by showcasing alternative governance models. To counter these threats, societies must draw from past successes, prioritizing inclusive policies, transparency, and civic empowerment. Democratic renewal demands continuous effort and adaptation, ensuring that institutions remain responsive to the evolving needs of their populace while adhering to core democratic principles.

Moreover, education plays a critical role in sustaining democratic momentum. By nurturing informed and engaged citizens, societies can strengthen their democratic fabric, equipping future generations with the tools needed to advocate for positive change. Civic education fosters an understanding of democratic processes, empowering individuals to participate actively and responsibly. It serves as a bulwark against misinformation and apathy, promoting a culture of vigilance and accountability essential for democratic sustainability.

## Role of Civic Education in Democratic Renewal

In a world where democratic systems face increasing strain, civic education emerges as a crucial mechanism for nurturing informed and engaged citizens. At its core, civic education provides an understanding of democratic principles—a foundation essential for informed citizenship and governance. It equips individuals with the knowledge needed to comprehend governmental processes, rights, and responsibilities. Understanding these democratic principles isn't just academic; it's the cornerstone of meaningful participation in democratic systems.

However, traditional educational methods often fail to address modern challenges such as disinformation, which can skew perceptions and undermine democracy. Here, modernizing curricula with technology plays a vital role. By integrating digital tools and media literacy into education, educators can empower young people to critically assess information. This approach not only counters disinformation but also fosters youth engagement by connecting learning with the realities of the digital age. Technology-enabled learning environments encourage students to interact with diverse perspectives, analyze complex issues, and debate respectfully—skills integral to robust democratic participation. This modernized approach is supported by researchers like Biesta (Citation2011), who emphasize critical thinking and deliberation skills within civic education.

Moreover, civic education extends beyond classrooms to foster community service and local participation through real-world learning experiences. Service-learning projects, for example, allow students to engage directly with their communities, applying classroom knowledge to societal problems. These initiatives cultivate a sense of social responsibility and underscore the impact of individual contributions on community well-being. As Barbehön and Wohnig (Citation2022) illustrate, civic education's dynamic nature encourages students to preserve existing values while questioning and transforming them—a duality that stimulates active citizenship.

Effective civic education also addresses the disparities articulated by Levinson (Citation2012), bridging the 'civic empowerment gap' that often leaves underprivileged groups underrepresented in the political sphere. By providing training and resources, educational programs can elevate the voices of those from less privileged backgrounds, ensuring a more inclusive political landscape. Engaging in community service projects not only benefits society but also enhances personal growth and reinforces commitment to civic duties, thus fostering lifelong engagement.

Lifelong learning forms another pillar of effective civic education. As societies evolve, so too must our understanding of democratic engagement. Continuous education helps maintain civic interest and adaptability, equipping individuals with the skills necessary to respond to new challenges. Lifelong learning promotes resilience within democracy, encouraging sustained participation across generations. Given the rapid changes in global and local contexts, the need for ongoing civic education becomes even more pronounced, aligning with the assertions of Hoggan-Kloubert et al. (2023) about empowering voices in various spheres of influence.

Curricular innovations are crucial for creating impactful civic education. Incorporating current events, cultural studies, and interactive discussions can help learners connect academic theories to real-world situations. A curriculum that adapts to societal needs and technological advancements ensures relevance and effectiveness, making civic education a dynamic field that evolves in sync with the changing world. This approach aligns with critical and materialist theories that advocate for addressing power structures and promoting social justice (Brookfield, Citation2020).

Community engagement is integral in translating theoretical knowledge into practical skills. Civic activities like volunteering or participating in public forums enable individuals to apply what they've learned, thereby solidifying their understanding and commitment to democratic ideals. This participatory approach embodies the essence of democracy: collaboration and shared governance among informed citizens. Such practices bolster social cohesion and inclusivity, key tenets of a healthy democracy (*The Importance of Civic Education: Empowering Citizens | Enterprise Wired*, 2024).

Another significant aspect is promoting ethical decision-making through education. Understanding ethical considerations in civic life, such as justice and equity, prepares individuals to navigate moral dilemmas effectively. This focus on ethics ensures that civic action is guided by principles that foster the common good, aligning with Holst's (Citation2021) emphasis on values within adult education practices.

Furthermore, civic education should extend beyond national borders, cultivating a sense of global citizenship. In today's interconnected world, understanding global issues and their local impacts enriches civic competence. Individuals equipped with this knowledge are better prepared to contribute positively both nationally and internationally. Promoting responsible global citizenship underscores the importance of empathy, tolerance, and cooperation among diverse cultures and communities.

## Potential Policy Innovations

In the current democratic landscape, transformative policy initiatives are crucial for revitalizing liberal democracies across the globe. One of the most significant avenues is ensuring universal voting access, a cornerstone for any functioning democracy. Universal voting access proposals are designed to eliminate barriers that hinder citizens from participating in elections. These include measures like automatic voter registration, mail-in ballots, and extended voting periods, all of which make it easier for citizens to engage in the electoral process. By removing obstacles such as rigid registration deadlines and limited polling hours, these proposals aim to create a more inclusive electoral system, thereby strengthening democratic participation.

Policies to incentivize civic involvement and fund democratic education initiatives are equally vital. Civic involvement can be encouraged through various means, such as tax benefits for those participating in community service or initiatives that recognize civic engagement as a criterion for educational scholarships. Furthermore, funding for democratic education could introduce curricula that focus on democratic values, political literacy, and the importance of participation from a young age. Education programs could extend beyond traditional schooling by incorporating workshops, seminars, and community events that foster an understanding of governance and individual civic responsibilities. By embedding these principles early on, societies can cultivate informed and engaged citizens capable of contributing positively to democratic processes.

Additionally, transparency measures are fundamental to enhancing accountability and curbing governmental corruption. Transparency in governance involves open access to information about government operations, decisions, and financial expenditures. Initiatives such as public-access databases, transparency in funding political campaigns, and independent watchdog agencies play a pivotal role in this regard. For instance, freedom of information acts enable citizens to request information that should rightfully be in the public domain, thus holding decision-makers accountable for their actions. Transparent governance creates trust between the state and its citizens, making it less likely for corrupt practices to thrive unchecked.

Support for grassroots movements is another transformative policy idea that can significantly impact democracy. Grassroots activism brings voices from diverse and marginalized communities into the policymaking arena, ensuring broader representation in decision-making processes. Policies that facilitate the growth and sustainability of grassroots movements include government grants, access to public spaces for gatherings, and legal protections against reprisals. Such support empowers marginalized groups and amplifies their concerns, leading to more equitable policy outcomes. By fostering an environment where grassroots movements can thrive, democracies ensure that a wider array of perspectives and experiences contribute to shaping policies.

The emphasis on universal voting access is underscored by America's long-standing issues with disenfranchisement, particularly among minority groups. Despite philanthropic efforts to incentivize voting, democratic decline persists (Kleinfeld, 2022). The critical nature of this issue calls for robust strategies that address systemic barriers while engaging citizens across the spectrum. Effective strategies might involve partnerships between government bodies and non-profit organizations dedicated to voter rights and education, ensuring comprehensive outreach and support for voters in underrepresented areas.

Equally pressing is the need to incentivize civic involvement through policy innovation. Educational institutions play a significant role in this transformation, offering programs that motivate students to actively participate in democracy. The American Democracy Project, for instance, works towards improving civic learning and voter participation, supporting colleges in fostering informed and engaged citizenship (<i>Organizations Bridging Divides | Resources | the Morton Deutsch International Center for Cooperation and Conflict Resolution | Teachers College, Columbia University</i>, n.d.). Such models can inspire broader adoption of educational reforms that prioritize democratic engagement.

Transparency's role in combating corruption and restoring faith in governance cannot be overstated. In many countries, systemic corruption erodes public trust, impeding democratic processes. Implementing stringent transparency measures can help rebuild this trust by showcasing governmental accountability. Countries like Estonia have made strides with e-governance systems that reduce bureaucratic opacity and improve citizen access to information. These advancements can serve as benchmarks for other democracies striving to mend the relationship between state and citizenry.

Supporting grassroots movements aligns with a renewed focus on participatory democracy. Movements like the civil rights struggle in the United States demonstrate the power of collective activism in effecting social change. These movements necessitate policy frameworks that protect activists' rights to assembly and expression, allowing them to advocate effectively for causes that resonate within their communities. Acknowledging the potential of grassroots initiatives not only enriches policy discourse but also ensures that legislative measures reflect the lived experiences and needs of diverse populations.

## Empowering Citizens for Participation

In today's world, cultivating empowered citizens who actively participate in democratic processes is not just an aspiration but a necessity. To achieve this, several strategies need to be emphasized, beginning with advocacy workshops and mentorship programs. These initiatives play a critical role in preparing individuals for active engagement by providing essential skills and knowledge that empower them to navigate the complex landscape of democratic participation.

Advocacy workshops serve as an educational platform, offering practical training on how to engage effectively with political systems and make one's voice heard. Participants learn about the intricacies of policy-making, the importance of civic responsibility, and methods of influencing decision-makers. Workshops often simulate real-world scenarios, allowing individuals to practice advocacy techniques in a controlled environment. Mentorship programs complement these efforts by pairing aspiring advocates with experienced mentors who can offer guidance, share insights, and provide support based on their own experiences. This personal connection fosters a deeper understanding of democratic processes and instills confidence in individuals to take informed actions within their communities.

Building community networks is another vital strategy in nurturing empowered citizens. These networks act as a conduit for collaboration and fostering resilience against polarization. In an increasingly divided society, having access to a supportive network can encourage dialogue across differing perspectives and create spaces for constructive conversation. Community networks are composed of local organizations, interest groups, and individuals who share a commitment to collective goals. They provide opportunities for grassroots organizing and facilitate partnerships that enhance communal strength.

For example, neighborhood associations and coalitions focused on specific causes bring people together, enabling them to work collaboratively towards shared objectives. By prioritizing inclusivity, these networks challenge polarization and help bridge divides, promoting a sense of belonging and shared purpose among diverse community members. Such networks are instrumental in uniting people around common issues, demonstrating the power of collective action in effecting positive change.

Outreach programs targeting underrepresented groups are crucial for increasing diverse participation in democratic processes. Historically marginalized communities often face barriers to engagement due to socioeconomic factors, lack of representation, or systemic discrimination. Outreach initiatives aim to dismantle these barriers by actively engaging these groups and ensuring their voices are included in the democratic narrative.

Successful outreach programs often involve tailored efforts such as bilingual information campaigns, community forums, and culturally sensitive engagement strategies. By acknowledging and addressing the unique needs and challenges of different demographic groups, these programs create pathways for greater involvement. Moreover, they emphasize the value of diversity in decision-making, highlighting how varied perspectives enrich the democratic process. Empowering underrepresented communities through targeted outreach not only enhances democratic legitimacy but also ensures that policies reflect the interests and experiences of all constituents.

Legislative advocacy represents a direct avenue for citizens to influence policy and drive democratic reform. As individuals become more engaged through education and community involvement, they gain the tools needed to effectively advocate for change at the legislative level. Legislative advocacy involves organized efforts to shape public policy through direct interaction with legislators and other government officials. It encompasses activities such as lobbying, petitioning, and participating in public hearings to convey citizens' concerns and priorities.

Citizens engaged in legislative advocacy must understand the policy-making process, including how laws are proposed, debated, and enacted. Strategic communication skills are essential for articulating clear and compelling arguments, whether through written correspondence or face-to-face meetings with policymakers. Additionally, building alliances with like-minded organizations and stakeholders can amplify collective impact and strengthen advocacy efforts.

By equipping citizens with the knowledge and resources needed to engage in legislative advocacy, we empower them to hold elected officials accountable and champion reforms that align with democratic values. This active participation serves as a check on governmental power, ensuring that policies remain responsive to the evolving needs of society.

## Final Insights

The chapter delves into the pressing need for a revitalization of liberal democracy, exploring both historical precedents and contemporary efforts to achieve this goal. It emphasizes the concept of a 'third founding,' where equity and inclusion are prioritized to ensure democratic systems are more representative and participatory. The challenges in realizing such transformation are significant, as entrenched interests resist change, and political polarization creates divisions. Yet, through fostering active civic participation, dismantling systemic barriers, and leveraging technology, there exists potential for democratic renewal. Reflecting on historical examples, from the reconstruction era after World War II to South Africa's transition from apartheid, indicates that citizen engagement and institutional reforms can drive democratic progress despite adversity.

The chapter underscores the complexity of overcoming obstacles within current democratic systems, highlighting how internal and external pressures continue to threaten their stability. It stresses that while strategies like universal voting access, transparency measures, and support for grassroots movements present viable pathways, they demand relentless effort. The role of civic education emerges as crucial, preparing individuals to navigate these challenges and participate meaningfully. By engaging diverse communities and fostering dialogue across divides, there's hope for incremental improvements. However, achieving substantial democratic revitalization remains an arduous task, requiring sustained commitment and adaptation to ever-evolving societal needs. Despite the daunting outlook, the chapter calls for persistence and collective action to safeguard democratic values.

## Reference List


Britannica. (2019). *South Africa - The unraveling of apartheid | Britannica*. Encyclopædia Britannica. https://www.britannica.com/place/South-Afric a/The-unraveling-of-apartheid

*Civic Participation and Empowerment*. (n.d.). United States Institute of Peace. https://www.usip.org/guiding-principles-stabilization-and-reconstructio n-the-web-version/stable-governance/civic-particip

*Democracy in Crisis*. (2019, August 29). Civic Power. https://doi.org/10.101 7/9781108380744.002

Galston, W. A. (2018, April 17). *The populist challenge to liberal democracy.* Brookings. https://www.brookings.edu/articles/the-populist-challenge-to -liberal-democracy/

Hoggan-Kloubert, T., Brandi, U., Hodge, S., Knight, E., & Milana, M. (2023). *Civic lifelong education: fostering informed citizenship amidst global challenges and democratic transformations (Editorial).* International Journal of Lifelong Education. https://doi.org/10.1080/02601370.2023.2234133

Kleinfeld, R. (2022, September 15). *Five Strategies to Support U.S. Democracy.* Carnegie Endowment for International Peace. https://carnegieendowment. org/2022/09/15/five-strategies-to-support-u.s.-democracy-pub-87918

*Organizations Bridging Divides | Resources | The Morton Deutsch International Center for Cooperation and Conflict Resolution | Teachers College, Columbia University.* (n.d.). Teachers College - Columbia University. https://icccr.tc.c olumbia.edu/resources/organizations-bridging-divides/

*The Importance of Civic Education: Empowering Citizens | Enterprise Wired.* (2024, February 16). Enterprise Wired. https://enterprisewired.com/the- importance-of-civic-education/

*WikiFreedom - Your AI-Powered Encyclopedia of Unbounded Knowledge.* (2024). Freedomgpt.com. https://freedomgpt.com/wiki/strengthening-democrati c-values-and-participation

# Policy Responses to Democratic Erosion

Exploring policy responses to democratic erosion uncovers a complex landscape marked by the challenges faced by modern democracies. Across the globe, these challenges have intensified, as political systems grapple with issues ranging from electoral interference to the concentration of power in fewer hands. In recent years, these threats have become more pronounced, raising alarms about the future stability and resilience of democratic institutions. As these systemic vulnerabilities come to light, it becomes increasingly clear that many democracies are ill-prepared to effectively counteract the multi-faceted forces undermining their foundations. While some nations attempt to reinforce their democratic frameworks, others find themselves sliding further into authoritarianism, thus exposing the fragility that often underlies even well-established democratic systems.

The chapter delves into several key strategies intended to shield democracies from these emerging threats. It covers reforms aimed at enhancing the accountability and resilience of democratic institutions by addressing practices like gerrymandering and advocating for proportional representation. Measures to strengthen checks and balances within government structures are also examined, offering insights into how oversight mechanisms can be fortified. Additionally, the role of civic engagement and education programs is highlighted, emphasizing the importance of empowering citizens through increased participation and awareness. Furthermore, the chapter discusses transparency measures to combat corruption, supported by examples such as anti-corruption task forces and whistleblower protection laws. Finally, the complexities surrounding digital technologies and media integrity, along with socioeconomic policies aimed at supporting working-class families, are explored, collectively weaving a narrative of potential pathways and obstacles in preserving democratic integrity.

## Reforming Democratic Institutions

Addressing institutional reforms aimed at enhancing democratic resilience and accountability is critical in light of the threats facing democracies worldwide. A key component of such reform is ensuring electoral fairness, which serves as the backbone for a healthy democracy by ensuring that all citizens have an equal voice in the political process. Measures that focus on reorganizing district boundaries can mitigate gerrymandering, the practice of manipulating electoral district lines to favor specific political outcomes. Gerrymandering distorts representation and often results in policy decisions that do not reflect the electorate's true desires. Therefore, establishing independent commissions to oversee the drawing of fair district boundaries is one avenue to combat this issue.

Furthermore, advocating for proportional representation could enhance inclusivity by providing various groups with fair representation in legislative bodies. While single-member districts can sometimes lead to skewed outcomes favoring larger parties, proportional systems can better reflect a diverse electorate's preferences. Implementing ranked-choice voting is another method gaining traction. It allows voters to rank candidates by preference, which helps ensure that elected officials have majority support, thereby promoting broader representation.

Strengthening checks and balances within government structures is also essential for preventing power consolidation and abuses of authority. By fortifying oversight mechanisms, governments can ensure they remain accountable to their citizens. An effective oversight system might include empowering independent judiciary bodies to review executive actions. Such bodies must function free from political influence, upholding the rule of law impartially and protecting democracy from potential overreaches by any branch of government.

Moreover, reinforcing legislative oversight plays a crucial role in maintaining balance within governmental systems. Establishing bipartisan committees to scrutinize policies and actions can prevent dominance by any single party or ideology. This scrutiny should extend to budget allocations and emergency powers, where oversight is often weakened, allowing unchecked actions that may harm democratic processes. Attention to these areas could diminish the risks associated with power concentrations that threaten democratic integrity.

Another cornerstone of bolstering democracy involves boosting civic engagement initiatives. These efforts encourage active citizen participation, fostering trust between the populace and their governing bodies. Initiatives like participatory budgeting, which allow community members to contribute directly to decision-making on public spending, exemplify how citizen involvement can be increased. Digital forums and town hall meetings are additional platforms where citizens can engage directly with leaders and influence policy decisions.

Educational programs aimed at increasing civic literacy are fundamental to these efforts. By equipping citizens with knowledge about their rights and the workings of government, democracies can empower individuals to participate more meaningfully in governance. Such empowerment is essential in building a resilient society capable of navigating challenges and ensuring that diverse voices are considered in shaping future policies.

Additionally, implementing transparency measures is vital for enhancing public trust and reducing corruption. Transparency not only strengthens accountability but also ensures access to governmental data, thereby enabling citizens to make informed decisions. Governments can achieve this by enforcing open-data laws, making information readily accessible and understandable to the public. Transparent governance reduces opportunities for corruption by exposing misconduct to public scrutiny, leading to increased confidence in political institutions.

Anti-corruption task forces can further reinforce principles of transparency and accountability. Empowering these units to investigate and prosecute corrupt practices without interference illustrates a government's commitment to ethical governance. Additionally, whistleblower protection laws encourage individuals to report corruption by safeguarding them against retaliation, promoting an environment where transparency can thrive.

Public sector reform, focusing on meritocratic recruitment and promotion processes, is another path towards minimizing corruption and ensuring efficiency. Institutions that prioritize the appointment of competent individuals based on merit rather than patronage tend to perform better and maintain higher public confidence levels. This approach reduces instances of favoritism and inefficiencies that compromise democratic functions.

However, it's important to acknowledge the potential challenges digital technologies present in achieving these goals. While digitalization offers new avenues for engagement and transparency, it also poses risks, including misinformation and privacy concerns. Thus, careful planning and regulation around technology use in governance are essential to maximize its benefits while mitigating associated threats (UNDP Digital Guides - Strengthening Democratic Institutions and Processes, n.d.).

Finally, ensuring that media outlets operate independently and ethically is crucial for informed citizenry and democratic discourse. A robust framework that supports journalistic freedom and integrity protects against misinformation and sensationalism, ultimately aiding in the promotion of well-informed, engaged communities (Rodriguez, 2024).

# Technology Sector Regulation

In recent years, the intersection of technology and democracy has sparked intense debate, particularly concerning the potential threats posed by misinformation, privacy violations, and algorithmic control. As we delve into regulations aimed at mitigating these negative influences, it becomes evident that comprehensive policy responses are critical for preserving democratic integrity.

Content moderation policies emerge as a primary line of defense against the dissemination of harmful content online. Social media platforms, in particular, have become breeding grounds for disinformation and hate speech, which can undermine democratic discourse and polarize societies. A concerted effort is required to establish robust content moderation frameworks. The Internet PACT Act, for instance, proposes guidelines for interactive computer service providers to manage risk through good faith moderation practices (<i>Tech Policy Trifecta: Data Privacy, AI Governance, and Content Moderation | Bipartisan Policy Center</i>, n.d.). These frameworks must include technical standards and human review processes to ensure accurate detection and reduction of harmful content. Encouraging platforms to develop automated tools that flag inappropriate material while allowing for contextual human oversight can significantly curb the spread of false information online.

Equally crucial are data privacy regulations that protect user data from misuse for political manipulation. In an era where personal information is commodified, stronger privacy laws are needed to safeguard citizens' rights and build trust between users and technology companies. As noted by Freedom House, governments must avoid imposing arbitrary bans on social media but instead should focus on regulatory actions that align with human rights standards (Freedom House, 2022). Protecting individuals' data from exploitation not only prevents undue influence on election outcomes but also fosters a more transparent and accountable digital environment.

Algorithmic accountability is another essential component in addressing the technological challenges facing democracy. Algorithms increasingly determine what information users encounter online, often leading to echo chambers that reinforce existing beliefs and limit exposure to diverse perspectives. By requiring transparency in these algorithms, policymakers can mitigate their adverse effects. Legislation mandating regular audits and disclosures of algorithmic processes could help illuminate biases and inform corrective measures. This level of transparency empowers users to make informed choices about the content they consume and encourages platforms to prioritize diversity in information dissemination.

While regulatory measures provide a structural backbone for safeguarding democracy, promoting digital literacy among citizens is equally imperative.

In an age where digital interactions shape political understanding, equipping individuals with the skills to critically assess the information landscape is vital. Educational initiatives focusing on digital literacy can empower citizens to discern credible sources from disinformation. Such programs not only enhance individual capacity to navigate the digital world but also foster a culture of skepticism towards unverified claims, thus bolstering resilience against manipulative narratives.

The need for civic engagement initiatives cannot be overstated when considering holistic approaches to counteract technological threats to democracy. Initiatives designed to engage communities in decision-making processes help bridge the gap between citizens and governing bodies, instilling a sense of ownership and responsibility towards democratic systems. By involving communities in discussions surrounding digital regulation, governments can ensure that policies reflect the nuanced needs and expectations of the populace.

However, the path to implementing effective technological regulations is fraught with challenges. Policymakers must strike a delicate balance between safeguarding democratic values and upholding fundamental rights such as freedom of expression. Any legislation aiming to regulate online content must adhere to principles of legality, necessity, and proportionality, ensuring that interventions do not result in censorship or stifle open discourse. Moreover, the rapid evolution of technology necessitates adaptive regulations capable of addressing emerging threats without stifling innovation.

## Ensuring Media Integrity

In recent times, the integrity of journalism faces significant challenges as it navigates the waters of digital transformation and media plurality. The role of journalistic standards and ethics has never been more crucial in shielding democratic discourse from the adverse impacts of misinformation and sensationalism. To fortify trust, media organizations are increasingly urged to uphold ethical guidelines that emphasize accuracy, fairness, and transparency in reporting.

Historically, journalism has differentiated itself from other forms of media by adhering to rigorous professional codes of ethics. These codes act as a compass, guiding journalists in maintaining quality and accountability while encouraging investigative journalism—a necessity for revealing truths that safeguard democracy (*Digital Trust Initiatives: Seeking to Reward Journalistic Ethics Online*, 2023). Such principles are pivotal in counteracting the spread of false information, a task made challenging in an era where engagement, rather than truth, often drives content dissemination on social platforms.

Additionally, the financial sustainability of media outlets is under threat, largely due to diminishing advertising revenues, exacerbated by monopolistic control of digital ad markets by tech giants like Google and Meta (*Digital Trust Initiatives: Seeking to Reward Journalistic Ethics Online*, 2023). Therefore, exploring public funding models becomes essential. These models can offer a lifeline to ensure editorial independence and protect media organizations from compromising their values under financial duress. Public funding can provide a buffer, allowing journalists to pursue stories that matter without fear of economic repercussions or censorship.

To cultivate a well-informed populace capable of critical analysis and rational decision-making, media literacy programs need to be implemented widely. These educational initiatives empower individuals to engage with media content discerningly. By fostering skills such as critical thinking, audience members can better navigate a complex media landscape, distinguishing fact from fiction and supporting democratic conversation. Such programs not only enhance individual understanding but also contribute to a broader culture of informed citizenship.

The effectiveness of regulatory bodies in overseeing media practices plays a vital role in ensuring accountability and transparency within the industry. Strengthening these organizations is paramount. Robust oversight mechanisms can hold media accountable, minimizing unethical practices and promoting a culture of responsibility among news providers. Regulatory bodies must adapt to the evolving digital environment, where traditional media regulations might not suffice to curb the surge of misinformation and protect the public's trust in legitimate news sources.

Global initiatives like The Trust Project, NewsGuard, and the Journalism Trust Initiative exemplify efforts to restore confidence in the media by establishing and promoting adherence to internationally accepted journalistic standards (Digital Trust Initiatives: Seeking to Reward Journalistic Ethics Online, 2023). These projects aim to evaluate news outlets against defined benchmarks, encouraging platforms and audiences alike to prioritize trustworthy sources. By generating machine-readable signals that guide algorithmic content curation, these efforts strive to amplify the visibility of credible journalism online.

UNESCO underscores the significance of self-regulation and accountability as strategic priorities in building trust in media—especially in regions grappling with the information disorder induced by technological advances (Council of Europe Conference: UNESCO Highlights Importance of Self-Regulation & Accountability Mechanisms for Trust in Media, 2023). Encouraging press councils and media associations to adhere to high ethical standards can serve as a free-of-charge complaint mechanism for the public, increasing transparency in handling grievances related to unprofessional conduct.

Furthermore, engaging public forums can act as a guideline to foster direct communication between the media and its audience. This interaction allows citizens to voice concerns and participate actively in media-related decisions, enhancing accountability and bridging gaps in perception and trust. Additionally, strengthening civic education can further support these efforts by incorporating media literacy into school curricula, thus embedding the importance of ethical journalism in the foundation of society.


## Supporting Working-Class Families

Socioeconomic conditions are integral to democratic participation, as they influence an individual's ability to engage actively in the civic sphere. Various policy measures can be instrumental in enhancing these conditions, thus fortifying democratic participation.

One crucial strategy is advocating for living wage initiatives. At the core of this concept is the need to ensure fair compensation for work, which helps bridge economic disparities. By earning a living wage, workers gain financial stability, empowering them to actively partake in civic activities and decision-making processes. Economic security enables individuals to allocate time and resources toward such engagements, fostering a more inclusive society. Nonetheless, setting appropriate wage standards requires careful consideration of regional cost-of-living differences and industry-specific challenges, ensuring all workers benefit equitably.

Affordable healthcare access is another vital aspect of socioeconomic improvement directly linked to democratic engagement. When citizens have secured access to healthcare services, they can participate in public life without the looming burden of medical costs. The Affordable Care Act (ACA) has been a stepping stone in this endeavor, but its incomplete implementation across various states highlights the persistence of regional inequities in health coverage. Expanding Medicaid eligibility and strengthening federal health guidelines can bridge these gaps, as evidenced by the program's popularity even in states that resisted its expansion (Gaines et al., 2021).

Education and training programs play a pivotal role in preparing citizens for active democratic engagement. By expanding access to education and vocational training, we equip individuals with the skills necessary to navigate complex political landscapes. Such programs not only bolster one's capacity for informed participation but also enhance employability, thereby improving economic prospects and self-sufficiency. Emphasizing lifelong learning opportunities ensures citizens remain adaptable in an ever-evolving socio-political environment.

Alongside education, expanding social safety nets is imperative. Robust safety nets support families during economic hardships, serving as a buffer against poverty and social instability. Programs like Temporary Assistance for Needy Families (TANF) and Unemployment Insurance (UI) are key components that require continuous enhancement. Increasing their benefit levels, streamlining application processes, and integrating them into comprehensive support systems can significantly reduce barriers to access

(Gaines et al., 2021). This not only aids immediate survival but also promotes long-term political participation by mitigating the stressors that inhibit civic involvement.

The recent expansions of the Earned Income Tax Credit (EITC) illustrate innovative approaches that could become permanent fixtures in efforts to promote economic security. These expansions, under the American Rescue Plan, provide increased benefits to low-income workers, particularly those without children (Gigineishvili et al., 2023). Making such enhancements permanent would alleviate financial pressures on vulnerable populations, unlocking their potential for greater engagement in democratic processes.

Additionally, supporting unionization efforts can empower workers to negotiate better terms and conditions, directly impacting their economic well-being and ability to engage politically. The Protecting the Right to Organize (PRO) Act exemplifies legislative efforts aimed at bolstering collective bargaining rights, repealing right-to-work laws, and preventing worker misclassification. Such reforms foster an environment where workers can collectively advocate for their interests, enhancing their participatory agency within both economic and political spheres (Gaines et al., 2021).

However, in implementing these socioeconomic policies, it is crucial to consider the broader systemic and structural challenges intrinsic to democratic erosion. Policymakers must recognize the interconnected nature of these issues, aiming for holistic reforms that address root causes rather than merely alleviating symptoms. This requires collaboration across local, state, and federal levels to establish universal standards and practices that ensure equitable progress nationwide.

While attempts to improve socioeconomic conditions face significant hurdles, including political polarization and resource constraints, the pursuit of these policies remains essential for sustaining democratic values. By creating environments conducive to active participation, societies can robustly counter emerging threats to democracy, fostering resilience amidst growing global challenges.

## International Cooperation for Democracy

International alliances play a crucial role in promoting and sustaining democratic values globally. As democracy faces challenges from authoritarian regimes, international cooperation becomes essential to support democratic norms and institutions.

Transnational Democratic Norms serve as one of the foundational pillars in this endeavor. These norms involve advocating shared values among nations through robust international agreements. Such agreements can establish common ground on fundamental human rights, democratic governance, and rule of law principles. For example, the Universal Declaration of Human Rights and subsequent treaties have set global standards that member states are encouraged to uphold. These documents provide a framework for nations to adopt similar democratic practices, creating a unified stance against undemocratic actions by member countries. By adhering to these transnational norms, democracies can collaboratively pressure authoritarian regimes to reform, leveraging collective influence to make meaningful changes.

Support for Global Civil Society is another critical aspect in strengthening democracy worldwide. International NGOs and advocacy groups often lead efforts to promote best practices in governance. These organizations not only advocate human rights and democratic governance but also provide resources to local civil societies in struggling democracies. They offer training programs, facilitate exchanges, and support grassroots movements, empowering citizens to demand accountability from their governments. For instance, during crises like those seen in Myanmar, transnational networks have mobilized resources to sustain local movements and call for international recognition of shadow governments (The Role of Transnational Civil Society in Shaping International Values, Policies, and Law | Chicago Journal of International Law, 2024). Such initiatives help nurture the foundation upon which resilient democracies can be built, ensuring that future generations are well-informed and engaged in civic life.

Another significant strategy involves International Observers and Monitors who provide impartial oversight during electoral processes. By dispatching neutral observers to oversee elections, credibility and trust in the electoral processes can be substantially increased. Monitoring teams can flag inconsistencies, support fair election conduct, and deter potential fraud or manipulation. The presence of international monitors in controversial elections serves as a check against autocratic tendencies, reinforcing public confidence in democratic institutions. Past instances, such as the international monitoring during Kenyan elections, have demonstrated how critical neutral oversight can be in volatile political climates, preventing election-related violence and fostering peaceful transitions.

Crisis Response Frameworks are essential mechanisms for coordinated international responses to democratic backsliding. They involve developing comprehensive strategies for timely intervention when democracies falter. These frameworks establish protocols for diplomatic engagement, economic sanctions, and, when necessary, peacekeeping missions to restore democratic order. For example, targeted economic sanctions and arms embargoes have been employed by international bodies to prevent authoritarian takeovers and encourage democratic reforms (Office of the Director of National Intelligence - Global Trends, 2021).

Guidelines for non-fiction include the promotion of digital literacy, vitally important in the digital age where misinformation spreads rapidly. Educating citizens to critically assess digital information empowers them against disinformation, enhancing their role in a democratic society. Public funding for media ensures editorial independence, allowing media outlets to operate without compromising financial pressures, thereby supporting democratic discourse.

## Concluding Thoughts

In examining the strategies to safeguard democracy against emerging threats, this chapter has highlighted the urgent need for institutional reforms that enhance resilience and accountability. The focus on electoral fairness, proportional representation, and ranked-choice voting outlines ways to ensure more inclusive and representative democratic processes. Additionally, reinforcing checks and balances within government structures is vital to prevent power consolidation. Equipping citizens with civic literacy through educational programs is another critical step in building a resilient society. While advancements in digital technology offer new opportunities for engagement, they also bring challenges like misinformation and privacy concerns. Thus, careful regulation of digital tools used in governance is necessary to maximize their benefits without compromising democratic integrity.

Nevertheless, even as we explore these strategies, numerous obstacles remain. Despite efforts to implement transparency measures and boost civic engagement, there are underlying societal and structural challenges that persistently threaten democratic systems. The interplay between technology and media integrity further complicates efforts to maintain a well-informed citizenry, as does the need for socioeconomic policies that enable wider political participation. The path toward safeguarding democracy requires not only addressing these immediate threats but also fostering international cooperation and adherence to transnational democratic norms. The pursuit of these goals is fraught with political polarization and resource constraints, making it clear that bolstering democracy in today's world is far from straightforward.

# Reference List

*Council of Europe Conference: UNESCO highlights importance of self-regulation & accountability mechanisms for trust in media.* (2023). Unesco.org. https://www.unesco.org/en/articles/council-europe-conference-unesco-highlights-importance-self-regulation-accountability-mechanisms

*Digital Trust Initiatives: Seeking to Reward Journalistic Ethics Online.* (2023, September 21). Center for International Media Assistance. https://www.ci

ma.ned.org/publication/digital-trust-initiatives/

Freedom House. (2022). *Policy Recommendations: Internet Freedom*. Freedom House. https://freedomhouse.org/policy-recommendations/internet-freedom

Gaines, A. C., Hardy, B., & Schweitzer, J. (2021, September 22). *How Weak Safety Net Policies Exacerbate Regional and Racial Inequality*. Center for American Progress. https://www.americanprogress.org/article/weak-safety-net-policies-exacerbate-regional-racial-inequality/

Gigineishvili, N., Teodoru, I. R., Karapetyan, N., Ustyugova, Y., Houtte, J. van, Jonas, J., Shi, W., Arzoumanian, S., Tintchev, K. I., Tuuli, M., Saliba, F., Talishli, F., El-Said, M., & Brollo, F. (2023, June 8). *Strengthening Social Safety Nets*. Departmental Papers. https://doi.org/10.5089/9798400239175.087.A004

*Office of the Director of National Intelligence - Global Trends*. (2021, March). Www.dni.gov. https://www.dni.gov/index.php/gt2040-home/gt2040-deeper-looks/future-of-international-norms

Rodriguez, C. (2024, September 26). *An American Democracy Built for the People: Why Democracy Matters and How To Make It Work for the 21st Century*. Center for American Progress. https://www.americanprogress.org/article/an-american-democracy-built-for-the-people-why-democracy-matters-and-how-to-make-it-work-for-the-21st-century/

*The Role of Transnational Civil Society in Shaping International Values, Policies, and Law | Chicago Journal of International Law*. (2024). Uchicago.edu. https://cjil.uchicago.edu/print-archive/role-transnational-civil-society-shaping-international-values-policies-and-law

*Tech Policy Trifecta: Data Privacy, AI Governance, and Content Moderation | Bipartisan Policy Center*. (n.d.). Bipartisanpolicy.org. https://bipartisanpolicy.org/explainer/tech-policy-trifecta-data-privacy-ai-governance-content-moderation/

*UNDP Digital Guides - Strengthening democratic institutions and processes*. (n.d.). Digitalguides.undp.org. https://digitalguides.undp.org/guide/strengthening-democratic-institutions-and-processes

# Charting a Path Forward

C harting a path forward for democracy requires acknowledging the growing challenges threatening its foundations. As political polarization intensifies, societies are becoming increasingly fragmented. This deepening divide fosters an environment where hostility thrives, and productive dialogue becomes rare. The erosion of trust between citizens and their leadership only complicates matters further. Disinformation, rapidly proliferating across digital landscapes, exacerbates these issues by distorting public perception and influencing political outcomes. Together, these forces create a turbulent cycle of mistrust and disengagement, which threatens to destabilize democratic institutions on a global scale.

This chapter delves into the myriad threats endangering democracy today, examining how they interplay to undermine collective governance. With a focus on political polarization and disinformation, it outlines the mechanisms by which these phenomena corrode public trust and fracture societal cohesion. Proposed solutions emphasize actionable steps that stakeholders can take to stabilize and reinforce democratic structures. Through fostering cross-party collaboration and enhancing media literacy, there may still be hope to bridge ideological divides. Additionally, grassroots movements emerge as powerful agents of change, offering bottom-up approaches that complement policy interventions. By recognizing and addressing these entangled challenges, it is possible to begin repairing the damages and setting democracy on a more secure trajectory.

## Recap of Major Threats and Solutions

As we conclude this exploration into the pressing challenges facing democracy, it is crucial to synthesize our understanding of the threats that have been identified and the corresponding solutions proposed. One of the most significant issues undermining democratic institutions today is political polarization. This deep divide fragments societies, creating an us-vs-them mentality that hinders constructive dialogue and problem-solving efforts. As individuals become increasingly entrenched in their ideological positions, cooperation across political lines becomes nearly impossible, endangering the very fabric of democratic governance.

Another formidable threat comes from the rampant spread of disinformation. In today's digital age, social media platforms are often exploited to disseminate false narratives rapidly. Nefarious actors—ranging from state-sponsored entities to rogue individuals—use these networks to manipulate public perception, skew election results, and sow discord among citizens. The pervasive nature of disinformation erodes trust in essential democratic processes, such as free and fair elections, thereby weakening the pillars of democracy itself (*Safeguarding Democracy against Disinformation | German Marshall Fund of the United States*, n.d.).

These threats are not isolated; they are deeply interconnected, collectively degrading the public's trust in democratic institutions. Political polarization exacerbates the susceptibility to disinformation since individuals are more likely to accept falsehoods that align with their preconceived notions. Conversely, disinformation fuels polarization by distorting public discourse and reinforcing tribal loyalties. The cumulative effect of these threats creates a vicious cycle wherein distrust permeates society, leading to increased cynicism and disengagement from democratic participation.

Recognizing these intertwined threats invites consideration of multi-faceted solutions. One promising approach lies in fostering collaboration across divides. Encouraging dialogue between political adversaries can help bridge gaps and promote mutual understanding. Initiatives that bring together representatives from different ideological backgrounds to engage in constructive conversations can mitigate polarization by humanizing the "other" and highlighting shared values and goals. However, this requires committed effort from political leaders, civil society groups, and citizens alike to prioritize unity over division.

Another arena ripe for intervention is the fight against disinformation. Strategies here must be multifarious. It is essential to combine regulatory measures that hold social media companies accountable with grassroots initiatives that educate the public on media literacy and critical thinking. Grassroots movements have emerged as powerful agents of change in this context. These local organizations, often embedded within communities, wield the trust and credibility necessary to counteract misinformation effectively. By organizing workshops, developing educational materials, and leveraging community influencers, grassroots efforts empower individuals with the tools to discern fact from fiction (<i>Grassroots Strategies to Combat Election-Related Misinformation (SSIR)</i>, 2024).

The potential of grassroots movements to drive effective change cannot be overstated. These movements are uniquely positioned to address the specific needs of their communities, tailoring their strategies to resonate with diverse audiences. They provide a bottom-up approach that complements top-down policy interventions, ensuring that solutions are comprehensive and inclusive. Community engagement activities, town hall meetings, and collaborative events serve not only to combat misinformation but also to strengthen civic bonds and foster a culture of informed participation.

Importantly, addressing these challenges requires a commitment to raising awareness. Understanding the complexity of the threats demands public education campaigns to illustrate how seemingly disparate phenomena are interwoven in their impact on democracy. Awareness-building efforts should highlight real-world examples where polarization and disinformation have disrupted democratic processes, underscoring the urgency of implementing solutions.

Moreover, long-term commitment is necessary to sustain democracy in the face of evolving threats. Combating disinformation and polarization is not a one-time endeavor; it is a perpetual responsibility. As tactics shift and new technologies emerge, democracies must remain vigilant, continuously adapting their strategies to safeguard their institutions. Public and private sectors must work in tandem to support ongoing research, fund innovative solutions, and promote policies that reinforce democratic norms and values.

## Vision for a Reformed Democratic Future

In envisioning an optimistic future for democracy, we must first define what constitutes a robust democratic system. At its core, this involves comprehensive representation and firm accountability mechanisms. Representation ensures that diverse voices and perspectives are included in decision-making processes, bridging the gap between policymakers and citizens. Accountability, on the other hand, involves holding elected officials and institutions responsible for their actions, fostering transparency, and reinforcing public trust. These principles are crucial as they create a political environment where every citizen feels heard and valued, thereby strengthening the democratic fabric.

Our understanding of democracy is also intricately linked to civic engagement. Civic participation extends beyond casting votes; it requires active involvement in community and political activities. This notion aligns with "thick" forms of public engagement, as discussed in global forums and highlighted in numerous reports ((Democracy Innovations on Capitol Hill: Report from the First Annual International Legislators' Forum on Innovations in Democracy - National Civic League, 2023)). Such engagement acts as a foundational pillar for vibrant citizenship and demands continuous dialogue between citizens and government entities, ensuring that decisions reflect the needs and aspirations of the populace.

To cultivate civic engagement effectively, guidelines can play a pivotal role. These guidelines should focus on informing citizens about avenues for participation, from local town hall meetings to broader policy advocacy initiatives. Encouraging volunteerism and community involvement at various levels can help demystify the political landscape, empowering individuals to contribute constructively. Educational programs aimed at enhancing political literacy and critical thinking are essential components, equipping citizens with the knowledge required to engage meaningfully in democratic processes.

Institutional reform is another avenue through which democratic values can be reinforced. Strengthened institutions that embody democratic ideals are vital for sustaining long-term governance stability. These entail revisiting the structures and functions of existing bodies to ensure they are adaptable to contemporary challenges. Drawing on international practices, such as those observed in parliamentary exchanges, can provide valuable insights into innovative solutions that have been successfully implemented elsewhere ((NW et al., 2020)). Institutions must be receptive to change, embracing new technologies and methodologies that promote transparency and improve public service delivery.

The global perspective offers valuable lessons for nurturing democratic resilience. Observing how different countries address their unique democratic challenges provides a wealth of knowledge and inspiration. For example, participatory models employed in certain European nations highlight the potential for citizens to directly influence policymaking, enhancing both transparency and accountability (Democracy Innovations on Capitol Hill: Report from the First Annual International Legislators' Forum on Innovations in Democracy - National Civic League, 2023). By integrating these practices, democracies worldwide can evolve, becoming more attuned to the needs of their citizens and fostering a culture of inclusivity and openness.

This interconnectedness underscores the importance of international cooperation. Cross-border dialogues and partnerships enable the exchange of best practices and collaborative problem-solving strategies. Such collaborations strengthen not only individual nations' democratic processes but also contribute to a more stable and equitable global political landscape.

Embracing digital innovation further complements efforts to enhance democracy. With technological advancements transforming communication channels and information dissemination, democracies have the opportunity to become more inclusive and responsive. Digital platforms facilitate direct interaction between citizens and their representatives, breaking down barriers and enabling real-time feedback loops (NW et al., 2020). However, adopting these technologies responsibly is imperative, with considerations for privacy and ethical use being paramount.

As we chart a path forward, establishing a comprehensive framework for ongoing evaluation and improvement becomes essential. Periodic assessments of democratic health, using defined metrics, can identify areas needing attention and refinement. This process ensures adaptive and resilient systems capable of withstanding emerging threats. Community feedback mechanisms, supported by technological tools, offer practical ways to gauge public sentiment and measure institutional effectiveness.

## Role of Individual Action and Community Initiatives

In the contemporary landscape of democratic governance, individual and community efforts have emerged as pivotal forces in fortifying democratic institutions. Encouraging personal responsibility is fundamental to fostering democracy. Each citizen's daily actions and decisions contribute significantly to the larger fabric of democratic society. As individuals become more aware of their roles in this complex system, they can exert influence in myriad ways—from participating in elections to advocating for policies that reflect their values. Personal responsibility in democracy isn't limited to casting a vote every few years; it encompasses staying informed about local, national, and global issues and taking part in discussions that shape public policy.

Grassroots movements are another vital component in strengthening democratic frameworks. Historically, such movements have served as the bedrock of civic engagement, challenging status quos and demanding systemic change. By mobilizing citizens around common causes, grassroots initiatives give voice to those often marginalized in traditional political systems. These movements not only highlight pressing social issues but also galvanize communities to work collectively toward solutions. Their impact can be seen in transformative legislation or shifts in public sentiment, showcasing the power of collective action. Grassroots organizations often operate outside established political structures, fostering innovative approaches to advocacy. They utilize community networks and digital platforms to reach broader audiences, illustrating how localized efforts can generate widespread influence (Gohar Chichian, 2024).

Creating supportive environments for participation is crucial for sustainable civic engagement. To cultivate these spaces, communities must prioritize inclusivity and accessibility, ensuring that everyone has the opportunity to contribute meaningfully. This involves breaking down barriers—be they economic, social, or educational—that prevent participation in democratic processes. Community centers, libraries, and digital forums can serve as hubs that promote dialogue and collaboration, empowering citizens to engage on their terms. Furthermore, partnerships between government bodies and local organizations can amplify outreach efforts, bridging gaps between policymakers and constituents. By recognizing the diverse needs of their populations, communities can tailor participation strategies that resonate with all members, thereby reinforcing democratic principles (Hussey, 2021).

Empowerment through education and lifelong learning is another cornerstone of a robust democracy. An informed citizenry is better equipped to make reasoned decisions and hold leaders accountable. Educational initiatives should extend beyond formal schooling to include workshops, seminars, and discussion groups that address current events and promote critical thinking skills. Moreover, leveraging technology to deliver educational content can democratize access to information, allowing people from different backgrounds to learn at their own pace. Lifelong learning emphasizes adaptability and resilience, key attributes in navigating the evolving challenges facing democracies today.

Guidelines for cultivating these elements can prove invaluable. For individual empowerment, guiding citizens to recognize and act on their civic duties fosters a sense of ownership in democratic processes. Encouraging community initiatives requires guidance on organizing effectively and sustaining momentum over time. Creating supportive environments might involve guidelines on removing participation barriers and fostering inclusive dialogue. Lastly, guidance on education can help establish frameworks for continuous learning and engagement throughout one's life.

Incorporating these strategies into broader societal efforts ensures that democracy remains dynamic and responsive to its citizens' needs. While daunting challenges continue to test democratic institutions, the cumulative impact of individual and community actions provides hope and direction for the future. By emphasizing personal responsibility, harnessing grassroots energy, nurturing open environments, and prioritizing education, societies can create resilient democratic systems capable of withstanding both internal and external pressures.

## Monitoring Democratic Health and Progress

In our exploration of strengthening democracy, it is crucial to underscore the importance of assessing and monitoring its current state. Without regular evaluation, we risk neglecting key weaknesses and missing opportunities for enhancement. Establishing a framework for evaluating democratic health is an essential starting point. This framework should include various metrics that provide insight into the functioning and vitality of democratic institutions. By systematically tracking indicators such as voter participation rates, media freedom scores, and levels of political corruption, we can develop a nuanced understanding of how robustly democracy is operating. Such metrics offer tangible data that allows us to compare different time periods or geographical regions, highlighting areas in need of reform while also recognizing successes.

Periodic reviews conducted by civic organizations are another vital component in this process. Civic groups play an indispensable role in holding governments accountable and ensuring transparency. These organizations should consistently engage in thorough evaluations of democratic processes to ensure they remain participatory and representative. By doing so, they contribute to a broader culture of accountability where no institution or individual is above scrutiny. The recommendations from these reviews can serve as a powerful tool for advocating necessary policy changes or reforms at both local and national levels.

Community feedback loops must be entrenched within any assessment framework if genuine improvement is to occur. Creating channels for citizens to voice their concerns and suggestions empowers communities and ensures that the government remains responsive to the needs and aspirations of those it serves. Feedback mechanisms might include town hall meetings, digital platforms for public comment, or participatory budgeting initiatives. By valuing community input, governments can refine and innovate policies to align better with public interest. Furthermore, these interactions help to build trust between citizens and state, fostering more collaborative governance.

The deployment of technology enhances the capacity for comprehensive monitoring and assessment. Technological tools offer unprecedented possibilities to collect, analyze, and disseminate data on democratic performance. For instance, digital dashboards can aggregate real-time data on election fairness, legislative activities, and citizen engagement metrics. Online platforms also enable wider participation, breaking down traditional barriers to entry and making it easier for individuals to contribute to the democratic dialogue. Technologies such as blockchain can enhance transparency by providing immutable records of electoral processes or government transactions, minimizing potential for fraud.

For these efforts to succeed, specific guidelines should shape our approach. First, establishing metrics requires defining clear, objective criteria that accurately reflect democratic health. Metrics must be regularly updated to remain relevant and should involve broad consultation with stakeholders to ensure they capture the full spectrum of democratic activities. Second, regular assessments conducted by civic organizations demand a structured approach, where findings are routinely published and made accessible to the public to maintain momentum and focus.

Third, implementing community feedback loops necessitates building robust systems to effectively gather, evaluate, and respond to input from citizens. This involves not only creating spaces for communication but also integrating feedback into decision-making processes meaningfully. Finally, utilizing technology calls for ongoing investment in digital infrastructure and literacy to maximize engagement and ensure equitable access to technological tools (Mačiulienė & Skaržauskienė, 2019).

Despite these promising strategies, the challenges facing modern democracies are formidable. In many cases, political institutions are resistant to change, particularly when transparency threatens established power structures (<i>Complete Guide | Political Process Monitoring</i>, 2017). Similarly, civic organizations often face resource constraints and external pressures that curtail their effectiveness. Furthermore, the digital divide remains a significant obstacle, impeding equal access to the technological advancements needed for enhanced monitoring.

Addressing these issues requires a concerted effort across multiple fronts. Legislative measures may need to be introduced to enforce accountability and protect civic space. Increased funding for civic organizations, both through governmental sources and philanthropic endeavors, would strengthen their monitoring capabilities. Educational initiatives aimed at enhancing digital literacy would ensure that all segments of society benefit from technological innovations.

## Call to Action for Readers

In navigating the complexities of today's democratic landscapes, it's crucial to remember that each individual possesses the power to influence change. While large-scale systemic transformations can often seem daunting, they invariably begin with personal commitments to uphold democratic principles. At the heart of this endeavor is a willingness to reflect on one's role within democratic frameworks. Each citizen can contribute meaningfully, whether through voting, participating in public debates, or simply staying informed about local and national issues. By recognizing our potential impact, we can better understand how to support and reinforce the structures that uphold democracy.

Engaging with local communities forms a vital part of this process, as our towns and cities are the immediate environments where democratic actions bring palpable results. It's here, in these everyday contexts, that engagement strategies for community involvement become most tangible and rewarding. Community engagement is more than attending meetings or signing petitions; it involves active participation in shaping policies affecting our neighborhoods and lives. The idea is reinforced by initiatives like participatory budgeting, an approach that empowers residents to allocate public funds directly, improving transparency and trust (Hussey, 2021).

Furthermore, one effective strategy for fostering local involvement is forming or joining groups centered on common interests or concerns. Such collectives can amplify individual voices, ensuring wider representation and more significant impact when advocating for changes. As Sören Fillet points out, utilizing platforms that facilitate resident proposals allows citizens to place their ideas on government agendas, creating a direct line of communication between communities and policymakers (*Go Vocal*, 2024). These platforms nurture a sense of belonging and shared responsibility, crucial components for reinforcing democratic practices at the grassroots level.

Beyond mere local engagements, there is a pressing need for advocacy and mobilization on larger scales. Advocacy plays a critical role in highlighting issues, spreading awareness, and pushing for legislative or social changes. Whether it's through campaigns, writing articles, or organizing public events, advocacy ensures that essential topics remain on the public radar. Effective advocacy often requires building networks and alliances, mobilizing resources, and strategically disseminating information to gain broader public support. This mobilization can spur movements that drive significant societal shifts, illustrating the transformative power embedded in collective action.

However, the push for democratic enhancement shouldn't be reactionary—limited only to times of evident crisis. It must be sustained consistently, emphasizing the long-term commitment required to nurture healthy democratic systems. Often, the real challenge lies not only in addressing immediate threats but also in maintaining vigilance and effort once the urgency subsides. Engaging persistently with democratic processes ensures that temporary setbacks don't devolve into lasting damages. This means continually educating ourselves about democratic rights and responsibilities, supporting inclusive policies, and holding elected representatives accountable, even when circumstances appear stable.

Moreover, nurturing a culture of sustained engagement involves cultivating open channels for dialogue and feedback. Digital-first engagement methods have proven efficient, offering new avenues for continuous participation in policy-making. These platforms enable individuals to express viewpoints, suggest improvements, and respond to policy changes swiftly and efficiently. As highlighted by digital democracy initiatives, the normalization of such tools enhances transparency and fosters trust, further embedding democratic values within community consciousness (Hussey, 2021).

Ultimately, the path forward is inherently collaborative. Strengthening democracy necessitates efforts from all sectors of society—citizens, organizations, businesses, and governments alike. While individuals reflect on their roles and engage locally, institutions must simultaneously work towards inclusivity, representation, and accountability. Together, these actions foster environments where democratic ideals are both upheld and actively practiced.

## Wrapping Up

This chapter has delved into the intertwined threats of political polarization and disinformation that are eroding democratic institutions. These issues create a cycle where polarization makes people more susceptible to false information, and disinformation deepens divides. Acknowledging these dangers, we explored several solutions, like fostering cross-political dialogues and grassroots efforts to promote media literacy. Such approaches could help block false narratives and bridge ideological gaps if pursued with collective dedication. Yet, the road to implementing these strategies is complex and full of potential obstacles, demanding sustained efforts from individuals, communities, and policymakers.

While envisioning a path forward, it's clear that strengthening democracy requires more than isolated efforts. Institutional reform needs to adapt to contemporary challenges, and citizens must engage actively in democratic processes beyond voting. Technologies offer both opportunities and risks, necessitating responsible adoption. Despite the multifaceted strategies proposed, the persistent nature of these democratic threats reveals a daunting reality. Without continuous vigilance and adaptation, efforts may fall short, leaving democracy vulnerable to the forces it seeks to withstand.

# Reference List


*Complete Guide | Political Process Monitoring*. (2017). Ndi.org. https://process monitoring.ndi.org/complete-guide

*Democracy Innovations on Capitol Hill: Report from the first annual international Legislators' Forum on Innovations in Democracy - National Civic League*. (2023, April 20). National Civic League. https://www.nationalcivicleague.org/ncr-article/democracy-innovations-on-capitol-hill-report-from-the-first-annual-international-legislators-forum-on-innovations-in-democracy/

*Grassroots Strategies to Combat Election-Related Misinformation (SSIR)*. (2024). Ssir.org. https://ssir.org/articles/entry/grassroots-strategies-election-misinformation

*Go Vocal*. (2024). Govocal.com. https://www.govocal.com/blog/10-easy-ways-to-be-a-more-engaged-citizen

Gohar Chichian. (2024, September 16). *How does civic engagement affect society?* Catchafire.org; Catchafire. https://blog.catchafire.org/how-does-civic-engagement-affect-society

Hussey, S. (2021). *Why is Community Engagement Important?* Granicus. https://granicus.com/blog/why-is-community-engagement-important/

Mačiulienė, M., & Skaržauskienė, A. (2019, December). *Building the capacities of civic tech communities through digital data analytics.* Journal of Innovation & Knowledge. https://doi.org/10.1016/j.jik.2019.11.005

NW, 1615 L. S., Suite 800Washington, & Inquiries, D. 20036USA202-419-4300 | M.-8.-8. | F.-4.-4. | M. (2020, February 21). *Hopeful themes and suggested solutions.* Pew Research Center: Internet, Science & Tech. https://www.pewresearch.org/internet/2020/02/21/hopeful-themes-and-suggested-solutions/

*Safeguarding Democracy Against Disinformation | German Marshall Fund of the United States.* (n.d.). Www.gmfus.org. https://www.gmfus.org/news/safeguarding-democracy-against-disinformation

# Conclusion

In a world increasingly defined by complexities and rapid changes, the erosion of democratic institutions poses a daunting challenge that demands urgent attention. The very fabric of democracy is being tested, not just by isolated events but by deep-rooted issues that threaten its core principles. Acknowledging these factors is crucial if we are to mobilize public awareness and spark action toward preserving democratic values.

Political polarization has undoubtedly disrupted the foundations of civil discourse, once considered the bedrock of democracy. In many contexts, political dialogue has devolved into divisive rhetoric, effectively stifling opportunities for meaningful conversation and compromise. As public debates become more about shouting matches than exchanges of ideas, the ability of democratic societies to address collective concerns diminishes significantly. This breakdown in communication is not simply an inconvenience; it strikes at the heart of democratic governance, where diverse perspectives should collaborate toward common goals.

Social media platforms, intended as tools for connection, have paradoxically accelerated these divisions. While they hold the power to disseminate information rapidly, they also facilitate the spread of misinformation and foster echo chambers that reinforce existing biases. This new media landscape complicates public discourse, making it difficult for individuals to discern fact from fiction. As viral content prioritizes sensationalism over truth, attempts at bipartisan dialogue face significant obstacles, hampering efforts to bridge divides and find common ground.

Economic inequality further compounds these challenges, acting as both a catalyst and consequence of democratic decline. The widening gap between rich and poor undermines social cohesion and breeds disillusionment with democratic processes. Many citizens, feeling economically marginalized, perceive politics as a game rigged in favor of elites, leading to apathy or anger towards the system supposed to represent them. This disconnection can manifest in decreased voter turnout and, in extreme cases, civil unrest, as disenfranchised communities seek alternative means to express their grievances.

Addressing these threats requires more than acknowledgment; it necessitates a reinvigoration of civic engagement. Democracy thrives when citizens actively participate in its processes, ensuring that governance reflects the will of the people rather than a detached few. Encouraging civic involvement, particularly among younger generations, is essential to building resilience against the forces undermining democracy. Engaged citizens are more likely to advocate for equitable policies, demand accountability from leaders, and resist the allure of simplistic solutions offered by extremist ideologies.

Despite the pessimistic outlook painted by current trends, there remains room for hope and action. Recognizing and understanding the threats facing democracy is the first step toward combating them. By fostering an informed and active citizenry, encouraging open dialogues free from polarizing vitriol, and addressing economic disparities head-on, it's possible to rebuild trust in democratic institutions. The path forward will be challenging, requiring concerted efforts from all sectors of society – policymakers, academics, activists, and everyday citizens alike.

Ultimately, the survival of democracy relies on our collective willingness to confront uncomfortable truths and make difficult choices. It depends on recognizing the interconnectedness of political, social, and economic forces shaping today's world. Only through comprehensive strategies that embrace inclusivity, transparency, and empathy can we navigate the turbulent waters threatening democracy's future. By doing so, there's potential not only to preserve democratic norms but to strengthen them for future generations.

In concluding this exploration of democratic erosion, it's important to emphasize that while the picture may seem bleak, it is not without remedy.

History has shown time and again that democracy is resilient, capable of adapting and evolving in response to changing circumstances. Yet, such resilience is not inherent – it must be actively cultivated and defended.

This defense begins with education, equipping citizens with critical thinking skills necessary to engage thoughtfully in civic life. Educational institutions play a pivotal role in preparing students to navigate complex political landscapes and understand the implications of their choices beyond immediate benefits. By fostering environments where diverse opinions are valued and debate is constructive, society can nurture informed individuals prepared to participate in democratic processes meaningfully.

Moreover, addressing misinformation requires collaboration between governments, technology companies, and civil society. Developing policies that promote transparency and accountability on social media platforms is crucial in curbing the spread of falsehoods. However, regulation alone is insufficient if not accompanied by efforts to promote digital literacy among users. Educating the public about how algorithms shape the information they consume empowers individuals to approach online content critically, reducing susceptibility to manipulation.

Economic reforms aimed at reducing inequality are equally vital. Policymakers must prioritize measures that enhance access to opportunities and resources for marginalized communities, ensuring that economic systems support democratic principles of fairness and representation. Implementing progressive taxation, investing in public services, and bolstering workers' rights can contribute to a more equitable distribution of wealth and, consequently, restore faith in democratic institutions.

Finally, reinvigorating civic spaces where citizens can connect and collaborate across differences is essential. These spaces foster community engagement, creativity, and innovation, serving as incubators for ideas that transcend partisan divides. Supporting grassroots initiatives and local organizations dedicated to building bridges between disparate groups can reignite a sense of collective purpose and agency.

While challenges abound, each obstacle presents an opportunity to reevaluate and strengthen our democracies. It is up to us – the politically engaged, academics, policymakers, and ordinary citizens – to decide whether democracy continues to erode or emerges renewed. Let us lean into this moment with courage and determination, acknowledging the weight of responsibility on our shoulders but also embracing the potential for transformation.

In writing this book, my intent was not merely to highlight the fragility of democracy but to inspire reflection and action. May it serve as a call to arms for those who believe in the enduring promise of democratic ideals and are committed to safeguarding them for future generations. The road ahead may be fraught with challenges, but together, we possess the power to forge a path toward a more just, inclusive, and vibrant democratic future.